D0261831

THE GLORY IN THE GREY

THE
GLORY IN THE GREY

FORTY-TWO TALKS ON EVERY-DAY
LIFE AND RELIGION

BY THE REV.
ARCH. ALEXANDER, D.D.

SIXTEENTH EDITION

ALLENSON & CO., LTD.
7 RACQUET COURT, 114 FLEET STREET
LONDON, E.C.4

MADE AND PRINTED IN GREAT BRITAIN BY
EBENEZER BAYLIS AND SON, LIMITED, THE
TRINITY PRESS, WORCESTER, AND LONDON.

TO

MY MOTHER

"For note, when evening shuts,
   A certain moment cuts
The deed off, calls the glory from the grey:
   A whisper from the west
   Shoots—' Add this to the rest,
Take it and try its worth : here dies another day.'"
                                        BROWNING.

FOREWORD

IT sometimes happens, when we are dispirited, that God's gracious gift of reviving comes to us along a very ordinary channel—in the form, perhaps, of some tonic, heartening passage found in reading, or the "morning face" and cheerful greeting of a friend. That is often all that we need—when our hurt is not serious—to send us back with a new zest and courage to our tasks; and that is the sort of usefulness which is desired for this book.

It does not pretend to deal with the great themes or the great hours of the religious life, but only with some of its simple encouragements and ideals for every day. There is a wide difference between the far-off flash of guidance which the sailor steers by in the darkness, and the humbler lights on board by which he sees to do his work. Yet he needs them both.

I desire to thank the publishers of *The Expository Times* for permission to include " The Odour of the Ointment," which appeared in that magazine some years ago; and the proprietors of *The Glasgow Herald* for a similar courtesy with regard to " The Shepherds, the Child, and the Wise Men."

ARCH. ALEXANDER

AYR, *September* 1914

CONTENTS

" And the vessel that he made of clay was marred in the hand of the potter : so he made it again another vessel, as seemed good to the potter to make it."

(JEREMIAH xviii. 4.)

I

GOD'S SECOND-BEST

A CERTAIN tree I once knew well, growing tall and straight on a windy height, had its top broken off in a gale ; and as I passed that way I said, " Wounded and half dead, that tree is done." But, as spring followed spring, I found that it was not so. The tiny, green shoots, round where the break had been, grew thicker and stronger year by year, till, by and by, a stranger could hardly have told that it had been broken. True. it was not the tree it had been, but it was big and high and leafy as before. So I learned that when the best is gone for ever, Nature has a second best in store, and with marvellous patience brings it out of her treasury.

In the potter's house, Jeremiah saw a vessel spoiled in the workman's hands through some flaw in the stuff, reshaped and moulded into another form—the best that could be made with such clay. In such a homely school was the prophet taught a new hope for men. Blindly and perversely do they squander and spoil the

11

gift of God ; yet is their case not hopeless if they but leave themselves penitently to His merciful repairing. God will make of them still vessels unto honour. Though innocence be gone, God's grace can still make a saint.

Jesus is this same Eternal Word of God, with hands and feet and a loving human heart. Drawn by His compassion, sinners, men and women who knew themselves failures, came to Him, and went away convinced that even for them life still held blessed possibilities. Jesus persuaded men that God was very willing, however marred their past had been, to help and heal them still. He never belittled failure. He never spoke lightly of sin. Yet He is our surety for the blessed hope there is for spoiled lives in the patient Hands of God.

Sometimes we claim God's promises on the heights, and forget that they hold in the valleys. So I want to bring the thought of our Father's loving resourcefulness—to which nature and prophecy and Christ have borne witness—down to homely levels.

I should like to speak of God's great storehouse of reserve blessing to those who feel that they are growing old. To the man who fears that, with his youth, he has left behind him everything worth having, I want to say that

God has other gifts still. Youth does not exhaust our Father's bounty. God has a gracious
Second-best for those who are ageing wisely. We
are all ageing, but some are growing towards
hope and faith and a deeper need and a deeper
experience of God. And that is not, in any sad
sense, to grow old. The spirit that is in living
touch with God's Spirit does not age like the body,
for God never grows old. What if the hair be
white then? Is it not written—" They shall walk
with Him in white because they are worthy?"

I am often tempted, too—though in this I
trespass, I fear, upon the domain of my brother
of medicine—to speak about God's Second-best
to those whose range of living has had to be
narrowed, to those who, though not seriously
ill, have had to surrender many of the liberties
and privileges of health. Even so, my brother,
life need not be wholly sad or bitter. Not a little
of the world's best work is done by its courageous
invalids. God has His gifts of quiet happiness
even for those who have had to take a smaller
house. Reckon up all you have left still, and
believe that God is very willing to help you to
the blessings which He keeps for His lame and
hindered children. That there are such is quite
certain. And some whom you know have found
them.

But the great comfort of this doctrine is for those who have failed. Now, there are failures and failures. One may fail, and try again, and get what he aimed for at the first. But there is a failure that is final, that shuts the door and turns the seeker down some other way, to bear the stigma—unsuccessful.

Yes, but how ? Embittered, hopeless ? Surely not, with this word of God to encourage us. Even for the failures, God has a Second-best. There are many who have found the blessing that lies beyond failure. Like the oyster, they have healed their hurt with a pearl. For, often and often, this Second-best of God's seems richer and more precious than what was lost. As a matter of fact, " Second-best " is a purely human measurement ; on God's scale it is really " better still." Oliver Goldsmith failed in his examination for the unambitious post of hospital mate. But out of that failure came a great gain to English literature. The Second-best, in God's good providence, for Goldsmith and for us, was " The Vicar of Wakefield." There is, in truth, no longer or more interesting chapter in the history of human effort than that which tells of the triumphs and successes that have been won out of failure. Let no one who counts himself a failure regard that as the end of the story. There is a wonderful Second-best waiting for him in God's keeping, if he gets up to try again.

> "Though deep in mire, wring not your hands and weep;
> God lends His arm to all who say ' I can.'
> No shamefaced outcast ever sank so deep
> But he may rise, and be again a man."

" They that wait upon the
Lord shall renew their strength.'
(ISAIAH xl. 31.)

II

ON WINDING UP A CLOCK

SOME people object very strongly to a clock in a bedroom, on the ground that it " murders sleep." Others of us, however, are prepared to justify its presence there, if only that it gives an official sanction occasionally to an extra ten minutes in the morning, and lends that luxury thereby a more exquisite edge. The starting-point of what I wish to say is a certain bedroom clock.

It is a modern, and a very cheap version of that picturesque, old-fashioned time-keeper which our fathers called a " wag at the wa'," but it works with a spring and a key. The only notable thing about it is that its spring has a range apparently of just a little over twenty-four hours. Consequently, when one retires after an unusually late sitting, the clock is to all appearance very far through. Its tick is of the most languid and feeble character imaginable. Like poor Joe's cart in " Bleak House," it goes labouring and groaning up the hill, seemingly on the very verge of breakdown.

16

I am always glad to remember, when I observe these signs of diminishing vitality, that I have such an effectual restorative at hand in the shape of a key. A few turns, and behold what a transformation! In any proper clock, the revival wrought by the key is staid and respectable. But this cheap bit of brasswork indulges in perfect transports of delight. It becomes ostentatiously vigorous. So brisk and hearty is it now, indeed, that it swings its little pendulum too far both ways, and, as Kipling's Macandrew said about his engines, " it knocks a wee."

If a clock can speak at all, the tenor of its remarks on these occasions is, " Well, there is such a thing as being very far down, and getting right and happily up again." Many a night I have listened to the little sermon which my few shillings-worth of clockwork has preached to me on the possibility of renewal, of rising up and beginning again in a new hope and strength and confidence. I should like to write that message now to all who have need of it. To the downcast, weary, and dispirited I would say, My brothers, God too has a key. God has a key.

After all, isn't that what happens as often as not with these bodies of ours? We used to hear a good deal of the " vis medicatrix naturæ," the healing power of Nature ; and it would do us all

B

no harm to remember that there is such a thing, and trust it more confidently and hopefully than we sometimes do. Men and women, as well as clocks, get run down ; and then life drags a bit wearily, and the grasshopper is a burden. But for all that, they don't die. Because, you see there is the key ! Somehow or other it finds them, is fitted in and turned round, and—behold the miracle of renewal ! You may call it a rest by doctor's orders, or a holiday, or a change of diet. You may discover that you want more exercise, and turn over a new leaf. The key may even be stamped and labelled in a chemist's shop ! The great point is that there is a key, and that it is not usually very hard to find. Getting wound up again is just as real a fact as getting run down, and quite as probable. So that, when one comes across a friend palpably out of sorts, it's a safe kindness to bid him cheer up because there's such a thing as a key, and the chances are that he— or his doctor—will find it. Remember that God's Will, Nature's will, is for our well-being. The moment we make ourselves unwell by our own indiscretion, Nature sets about repairing the damage. The sick man's wisdom, therefore, is to trust quietly and confidently to those bene-ficent powers of Nature that are all on his side.

Those who work with their brains, too—and

most people have to do that nowadays—sometimes find that the mind goes off duty. There are days when the student reads a page of some book right through, and can tell nothing whatever about it. Again, and, it may be, soon afterwards, ideas seem to leap out at him from every line he reads. Another case of winding up! Somewhere, between these two days, an unseen hand has fitted in the key, and his strength of mind is renewed. When your mind has struck work, do not be unduly anxious. Remember the cheerful philosophy of the key, and forget not that, on this plane also, a few turns of that can make a wonderful difference.

And don't we all know that there is such a thing as getting run down in the realm of the spirit-life, when faith seems to grow cold and one does not care to pray, when the lights burn low, and the ideal of Jesus appears to have lost its attraction? Robertson of Brighton sometimes wrote letters in which he declared what a poor thing he found the ministry to be, and how little suited he was for the office. His biographer explains that these letters were almost all written on Mondays. On Mondays, mark you. Spritual rundownness is sometimes due to a merely natural reaction. You can't always keep your soul at high tension. There is such a thing as spiritual appetite, which, like the physical, goes and comes again.   Or it may be due to neglect of the laws of spiritual health.   If your higher life is not being nourished, you cannot expect it to be healthy. Men who miss meals and take no exercise land themselves in trouble by and by.   If you starve your soul, or if you do not give your spiritual impulses an outlet in some actual practical effort, they will grow weaker, and your highest life becomes like a clock nearly run down.

But there is such a thing as a key for that trouble.   There is a spiritual revival possible for us all, not only in the midst of the years, but again and again and again.   Because—and this is the great truth I have been trying to guide you to from the beginning—" they that wait upon the Lord shall renew their strength."   That is the key.

In " The House of Quiet," A. C. Benson has a fine word-picture of the slow beginning of a much-needed shower of rain.   He describes how the trees and the flowers " seem oppressed with heaviness, yet trustfully conscious of the divine storage of that pure and subtle element that is taking place for their benefit," and how patiently and quietly they droop, and wait for God's rain.

The soul has its arid seasons too.   Its refreshment also comes from God.   And the wisdom that the flowers teach us is to wait, quietly, patiently, submissively, trustfully. Put yourself in the way of the great healing, restoring energies of God—and wait. With Him there is abundance of blessing. It is His pleasure to restore the faint soul, and make glad the heart that droops. There is a key, my brother; never doubt there is a key, and, by and by, your hope and faith and zeal for service will come to you again. Wait upon the Lord, not anxiously, nor in tense expectation, but as the tree waits for the shower, or as the child waits for his father, perfectly sure that though he seems to have left him for a while, he has not forgotten him, and, in due time, will return to make him glad with his countenance.

III

THE ODOUR OF THE OINTMENT

IN Browning's " One Word More," addressed to his wife, he compares himself to the artist Rafael who tried, in poetry, to utter the love that filled his heart. Browning wishes that he, too, could express his love more fully by some other art than his own, since his poetry did not, and could not, tell it all.

It was in some such way Mary felt when she broke her alabaster box of ointment at the feet of her Lord. Speech was not enough. When in an abandonment of gratitude she poured out all the contents of her precious casket, she was trying in her own way to say the One Word More which cannot be spoken, but which Love has been trying to speak since ever the world began.

I want you to think of that incident, and especially of these words in the story of it—" The house was filled with the odour of the ointment." For in that sentence we have hidden the secret of all winsome influence. This gracious act of Mary's, in its golden frame of Christ's acceptance and praise, is like a mirror in which we can see and compare the manner of our living and our loving.

First, let me ask you to note the reason of this widespread fragrance.   It lay, we can see at once, in the fact that the box was broken and all the contents spilled out.   If Mary had done what the disciples wanted her to do, she would have poured out just enough for the anointing.   She would not have broken the box.   She would have kept some for another occasion.   And Christ would have been anointed just the same, and the balance might have been given to the poor, but, ah, the fragrance would not have filled the whole house !

Mary, I say, might have done this, and no one could have blamed her, but it would never have been told for a memorial of her.   Don't let us say a single word against the doing of mere duty, against faithfulness up to the legal limit, for even that is none too common.   But heaven help us, in our hour of need, if our friends do no more for us than that !   There are good and estimable people who quite approve of the disciples' criticism of Mary, and themselves keep a tight hold upon all superfluities.   They perform their social and religious duties with faithfulness and precision like a machine.   But somehow, the broken-hearted in need of healing, and the failures who need mercy are not drawn to their doors. They live correct lives and they are righteous people, but they do not attract. There is no widespread fragrance there.

But there are others, frail and imperfect, in many ways perhaps, who possess an irresistible charm, because not duty but love rules in their hearts. These are the people who break their alabaster boxes and give what they have without stint or calculation. They live on Christ's second mile. Those in trouble seek them out by the same instinct that takes the bees past the corn and the grasses on to the heather and the flowers. These are the men and women whose lives are fragrant, for the secret of a gracious influence is just self-forgetfulness and the power that casts out self is love.

Notice, secondly, the service of the widespread fragrance. Mary's act was meant for Jesus only. The love and gratitude of which it spoke were for her Master and Friend alone. But she could not prevent the odour of it stealing all over the room and refreshing the disciples also with its sweetness. She ministered to more than the Christ.

That is always true of acts like Mary's. Never a man or woman yet made offering of testimony or service to Jesus Christ, and for love's sake poured all at His feet, but the sweet savour of it reached all those also who were near. You never break your box for one only, even when you break it for Christ. We have seen some brother, bowed down by a sudden blow, take up his cross humbly and patiently, and return with a brave heart to his labours again. We have heard the mourner steady her voice to ask through her tears how some ailing neighbour did. Though we knew that the brave front and the self-forgetting were for Christ's sake, given without thought of us, yet into our hearts also, who only stood by and saw, the fragrance of these offerings stole, to linger, like a breath of heaven, for many a day. It is a law of God that you can never deprive a loving deed or a Christ-like action of its influence. Every time you forget yourself in Christian charity or in the service rendered for love's dear sake, you are speaking to a bigger audience than you know. Not only is your Lord's heart made glad, but we also, your neighbours, who see to what brave lengths love carries you, or how sorrow only makes you more tender, we, too, are made better men and women by the sight. The savour of your act invades our lives also, and purifies and enriches them. That is always true, even though you know it not.

Thirdly, I would like you to think out the exact details of the spreading of the fragrance of Mary's ointment over the whole house, for I am sure that there, most of all, the story has its lesson for you and me. In the upper room the company was gathered, and there the rare offering of Mary's love to Christ was made. In the upper room. But the odour of it filled more than the room. It filled the whole house. Downstairs were the common rooms where the ordinary occupations of daily living were carried on—the kitchen and the cooking place where the hard, rough work of the household was done. The odour of Mary's ointment in that upper, inner chamber was felt. mark you, even in the common rooms and work-places downstairs. It reached and sanctified even them.

Do you see what a fine sermon there is in that ? How shall we know, how can the world judge of the homage and worship which a man offers to Christ in the inner chamber of his heart ? Is it enough that he counts himself, and professes to be, among those who give Him honour there ? It is not enough. There should be outward tokens. The influence of his offering of himself to Christ in the temple of his heart should fill his whole life. The fragrance of his prayer and fellowship and thankfulness should be felt down

even on the common daily levels of his life, in
the places where he earns his bread and plies his
calling and meets and deals with his fellow-men.
He should be a different man on the street and
in the market-place because he loves the Christ
and worships Him in the sanctuary of his heart.
It is for this that the world looks and watches,
and has a right to look and watch—ay, and to
point the finger when it does not find it. For, as
it was written of Christ Himself that " He could
not be hid," so may it be affirmed of all real heart
homage to Christ. That cannot be hidden either.
The odour of it, as of ointment poured forth, must
reach down even to the counter and the office
and the living rooms of home. That is the ultimate test and the hardest test of a man's religion.
God send us more Christians whose holy places
scent and flavour and sanctify each common
day and all its ordinary business ! God help us
to answer better to that test ourselves !

IV

LITTLE SANCTUARIES

In a very beautiful passage in Ezekiel, God declares, by His prophet, that though the exiles
were far from their own Temple and scattered
abroad, yet He would be to them as a little
sanctuary in any place to which they might come.
We need to remember that, besides His ordinary
and public means of grace, God has for each of
us private ones. We, too, have our brooks by
the wayside, our little sanctuaries, where God
meets with us.

One of the most striking features of the communion of the saints of the Bible with their God
was the homeliness, the everydayness of it. It
was as he went upon his way that Jacob met his
angel. It was while he sat at his tent-door that
Abraham found God draw near. Not even in
the New Testament was the disciples' fellowship
with Christ confined within Temple precincts
or within one specially sacred day. Their inter-
course with the Master was as broad and as long
as their life. Lake, hillside, garden, fishing,

28

dining, preaching—these were all holy places and occasions, for Jesus touched them and had to do with them all.

Now that is not possible for us, of course. We cannot meet Him in human form by the wellside when our day's work is done. But I think we forget that though there is one day sacred to Him, and one place where He has promised to meet with His people, He is with His friends all the days, and claims our loyalty and our service over all the breadth of life. A man's office can be a little sanctuary, not because he formally prays or reads his Bible there, but because he tries there to do justly and to love mercy and to follow Christ in his calling as a business man. Home is, for many, one of God's little sanctuaries, and in its quiet love and service He is loved and served. For nearly everyone, Nature becomes at times a temple of the Most High, when the ancient, ever-lasting song of brooks and streams, or the sough-ing of the woods, or the long wash of the sea become ministering voices that call us in reverence and worship nearer to His Presence.

There is no place, indeed, too unlikely to be a meeting-place with God. Peter found that God's sanctuary was sometimes a prison ; Paul found that it was sometimes a desert. As a man reads quietly by himself, the Spirit of God may touch him so that he sees things which it is not lawful to utter. On the other hand, some have confessed that they have learned more about God from poor and simple folk than in all the books they ever read. There was a room in Daniel's house that was nearest God because its windows opened towards Jerusalem: yet Isaac's little sanctuary was not within builded wall or tent at all, but in the field at the eventide. And I have heard a man say that never in all his life had he a clearer sense of the presence of God than on a certain cold morning in winter when he sat in the corner of a third-class carriage on a branch line in Ayrshire.

A sick room is a dreary place to think about, abhorrent to the healthy-minded, yet, to many hundreds that has been a little sanctuary indeed, where God met them and blessed them, filling them with a new joy and purpose in living such as they had never cared to know in days of health.

Don't let us be surprised though our brother's little sanctuary should seem to be in a strange place. Remember Lowell's fine message :—

> " To each in His mercy hath God allowed
> His several pillar of fire and cloud."

But, besides honouring our brother's sanctuary, let us cherish, and be thankful for, our own. To see a soul of goodness even in things evil is a covetable gift. But, if I might, I should ask another, for all who read this, and for myself— the gift to go through the ordinary days, and every now and then to find a shrine ; the gift to understand that when my heart burns within me, it is no ordinary Traveller who has joined me by the way ; the grace to be thankful for all that I have learned of God within His little sanctuaries, and the faith to expect—to-morrow, any day— to come upon another.

*" But Peter said, Not so,
Lord ; for I have never eaten
any thing that is common or
unclean."*

(ACTS x. 14.)

V

IMPOSSIBLE BREAD

WHEN Peter saw, in his vision, a sheet let down
from heaven in which were all manner of beasts,
and when a Voice said, " Rise, Peter, kill and
eat ! " the Apostle replied, " Not so, Lord ; for I
have never eaten anything common or unclean."
He demanded, in God's provision for his needs,
absolute compliance with his own sense of fitness.
Because the animals were not as Peter himself
would have chosen, he would not budge to touch
them.   Peter's attitude was, in homely phrase,
" sticking."   He was over-prudent, too particular.

De Quincey said a very clever thing about
Coleridge which exactly describes this attitude.
He said Coleridge "wanted better bread than
could be made from wheat."   It is a spirit which
is common.

We can see it, for example, in social life.   In
Ian Maclaren's " Kate Carnegie " we are told
how young Carmichael used to be afflicted with
a mood of supercilious disdain for the other
students of his year, finding serious faults in them

all. But the mood would pass, and he returned to wisdom, recognising that his fellows were not such a bad lot after all, " above all, recognising," says his shrewd biographer, " with what imperfect instruments the work of the Church had always been done." That sentence might almost be framed and hung in all our Church Meeting and Committee Rooms. Yes, the work of the Church has always been done by imperfect instruments, but it *is* done, thank God. We have all our faults and failures and fads. This one of us is almost sure to get hold of a new thing by the wrong end from the first, and oppose it blindly. That one may be trusted to take up a new scheme enthusiastically, and drop it half-way. In similar fashion we might label all our fellow-workers ; and they, of course, might label us.

What, then ? Why, recognise the fact, frankly, fully, once for all, and go ahead nevertheless. Make the best of what you have. It would be perfectly delightful if we could always get everybody to agree with us, and do things in our way, but we can't, and that's the end of it. To demand it, is simply to ask better bread than can be made from wheat. To stand out of a plan because you would not do it in that way, to refuse your help to a project because, in your view, it has been wrongly gone about, is very natural,

c

but it is just exactly the attitude from which the Lord had to persuade Peter. " Not so, Lord," you are saying to the Master who has called you to lend a hand in some good cause. " Not so, Lord, for I have never been accustomed to do things in this way, and there are features in the proposal of which I do not approve." It looks silly on paper, doesn't it ? The trouble is that it is so common in actual life.

Again, we may see the same spirit at work in Home Life. There is nothing morally finer than a passion for perfection. But it must be for one's own perfecting. A passion to have others perfect, to have one's surroundings or home perfect, is merely the outward index of a prig. One has heard of men for whom the sun went down at mid-day because their meal was not on the table exactly to the minute. Wesley, as W. L. Watkinson relates, tells that one day, when he was sitting by the study fire of a very wealthy gentleman, a puff of smoke came down the chimney, whereupon the host plaintively addressed the evangelist thus : " You see, sir, I have to put up daily with this sort of thing."

Well, I suppose, in the perfect home, chimneys would never smoke, servants would never forget, wives, mothers, and sisters would never say the wrong thing. But those who in fretting and

fuming displeasure are postponing their happiness
till that ideal stage is reached are making a very
serious mistake. Happiness does not wait upon
perfection. Even amid occasional discomforts,
with things just as they are, you may be as happy
as the day is long. It's a great thing to be able
to take people and things as they are, not asking
them to be, not expecting them to be, absolutely
perfect. Such a demand is hardly fair, you know,
since you are scarcely perfect yet, yourself!

This spirit is most out of place in the sphere
of personal religion. Yet there are some who not
only ask that those who work with them should
be built to their precise pattern, but they ask
that God's plans should square with their ideas
and be such as they can understand and approve.
Stevenson has satirised this spirit finely in his
"Counter-blast Ironical," when he makes the
critic say :—

> " It's strange that God should fash to frame
>   This yearth and lift sae hie,
>   And clean forget to explain the same
>   To a gentleman like me."

Strange as it may seem, one tacit reason why
men do not yield themselves in trust and homage
to God is that they think He has not sufficiently explained Himself. His revelations are not
definite and insistent, like the summons of a

telephone bell. He does not show Himself unmistakably. He keeps silence. And the queer grudge that some men have against Him for that, is one of the reasons that keeps them from giving Him the full allegiance of their lives.

Others ask for a creed with no blanks and mysteries in it. They would do His will if they were quite sure of the doctrine, forgetting that the appointed order is just the other way about. So, insisting on conditions exactly to their mind, they wait and wait and come no nearer, and at last drift away through life without any strong helpful beliefs of any kind, without any experience of God at all, blown about by every wind of doctrine, caught, for a while, by every fashionable drift in turn, whether of faith or denial, but never getting into the line of the great Trade Winds of God that would blow them steadily and surely forward on their way.

He that regardeth the clouds shall not reap, says Ecclesiastes. And he who demands better bread than wheat will make is never likely to get very much to eat. Far wiser and better is it just to make the best of things as they are. Help the good cause forward, though it has not been engineered as you would like. Work loyally yourself, though your fellows are a bit trying at times. Thank God every day for the priceless gift of home and human love, and do not let an occasional smoky chimney spoil your happiness. Rejoice that you have heard Jesus calling you into Sonship, and yield yourself and go, leaving your problems and difficulties to be explained by and by. There are so many of us speaking thus of Christ our Lord :—

> " It were not hard, we think, to serve Him
>   If we could only see.
>   If He would stand, with that gaze intense
>   Burning into our bodily sense ;
>   If we might look on that Face most tender,
>   The brows where the scars are turned to splendour,
>   Might catch the light of His smile so sweet
>   And view the marks on His hands and feet,
>   How loyal we should be!
>   It were not hard, we think, to serve Him
>   If we could only see ! "

But how many of us have learned that this is Christ's answer—the only answer there is ?—

> " It were not hard, He says, to see Him
>   If we would only serve.
>   He that doeth the will of Heaven
>   To him shall knowledge and sight be given.
>   While for His presence we sit repining,
>   Never we see His countenance shining.
>   They who toil where His reapers be
>   The glow of His smile may always see,
>   And their faith can never swerve.
>   It were not hard, He says, to SEE Him
>   If we would only SERVE ! "

VI

LAUGHTER

It is a very strange thing that the tradition of
the Christian religion should be against laughter.
Somehow we gather from the teaching we receive
that laughter is a perilous liberty, an indulgence
hardly safe. We can imagine God very near
to the man who weeps, but we have been taught
to believe, one might almost say, that He must
be very far away from the man who laughs. Yet
as we get increasing insight into life and the
essence of Christ's religion, we feel that somehow
that is wrong. It is a strong tradition, with
many developments, but at bottom it is an
unhealthy and mistaken one.

It proceeds largely from the belief that Christ
Himself, our Lord and Master, discouraged
laughter and gladness ; that a mark of our discipleship therefore ought to be seriousness and solemn
gloom. Thus, Farrar, in his very popular " Life
of Christ," says, " We are never told that Jesus
laughed, while we are once told that He wept."
Now God forbid that even in our thoughts we

38

should take from the glory and honour of our
blessed Lord and Master. But is a saying like
that the whole truth about Christ ?

We are told that He was slandered by being
called a gluttonous man and a wine-bibber. And
it is difficult to see what earthly point there could
have been in such an accusation if His demeanour
was one to which a smile was unknown. Did not
He Himself declare that there was as much difference between His attitude to life and John's—
who was the typical ascetic—as there is between
a wedding and a funeral ? We read, in the
Gospels, of Jesus going to a marriage, and He
was a guest at feasts. He watched the merry
games of childhood with an interested eye, and
the little ones loved Him—a sure sign that He
was no kill-joy. Further, in the Gospels, there
are sayings of Jesus which an orthodox interpre-
tation finds it hard to explain unless on the
assumption that they show a vein of humour ;
and for all the deep seriousness of His words, is
it not natural to think that there was something
of that quiet laughter which is so nearly akin to
tears in Christ's eyes when He spoke of feeding
swine with pearls, of camels passing through the
eye of a needle, or of a man seeing a splinter in
his brother's eye but not perceiving the beam
that was in his own ?

The tradition that a religious man must always be grave and sombre, when it attempts to justify itself by the example of Christ, can do so only by taking a one-sided view of His Person and character. Certainly a religious man will not be found, and ought not to be found, sharing in heartless frivolity, or the laugh at misfortune and pain in another. But that is a different thing from excluding sunshine and lightheartedness from religion altogether.

The more one thinks of it, the more one is convinced that laughter, as Sarah says in her doxology of motherhood, is a gift of God, like sunshine, and music, and love. God has given it a place in His scheme of things when He sets lambs racing and frisking in the spring-time, and children shouting with happiness in their play. It is only a perverted and morbid idea of religion that regards God as looking askance at the innocent and happy laughter of His grown-up children. Laughter indeed is sometimes our prayer of thankfulness to Him.

Moreover, laughter is one of the strongest reforming agencies in society. Lord Rosebery, with his usual felicity of phrase, reminded us, not so long ago, that our chief debt to Charles Dickens was that he taught us to laugh again. That is true, of course. But I wonder if you have

thought of all that Dickens did when he did that ?
It was not merely that he gave us excuse for the
wholesome physiological exercise of laughter.
For that alone, one may be grateful. But he did
more. He taught us, by making us laugh. He
reformed abuses and infused a kinder, more
humane spirit into English society, by making us
laugh. When Dickens wishes to enlist our sympathy for some ill-treated section of the community, little under-fed domestics, or shamefully
abused schoolboys in Yorkshire, he does not pile
on the agony. As Mr Chesterton would say,
he piles on the ludicrous. But what is the consequence ? Why, when the laughter has subsided,
there comes the swift reflection—But what a
shame it is for children to be treated so ! We
come to that conclusion ourselves, it has not been
thrust upon us by the writer, and therefore it is
tenfold more firmly established, and will be
kept in mind much longer. That is the justification of Dickens' humour as a moral force. Humour
is the cutting point that gives his message entrance.
After it is in, it does its own work. Many other
men besides Dickens felt strongly the abuses of
the time and struck at them savagely. But
Dickens laughed and joked as he plied his weapon.
Yet the things that he touched with it died out of
hand ! " The vein of laughing," says John

Milton, " hath ofttimes a strong and sinewy force in teaching and confuting." The Puritan is right ; and Charles Dickens is a proof of it.

Then, again, laughter is sometimes an index of moral character and self-government. When a man is made to feel some of the inevitable pin-pricks of life—the sudden angry word of a good friend, the perplexing conduct of a fellow-worker—which is the mark of the higher type of character, to laugh at the thing good-humouredly and go on one's way; or to worry over it solemnly, to demand an explanation, to write a letter, and very likely to blow the accidental spark into a pretty, good-going blaze before all is done ? We have no doubt of that. It is the man who laughs who wins.

So, the man who laughs at his fears is no longer very frightened. When you can laugh at your worries you have got above them. And when you can laugh heartily and happily at yourself, you are on the fair way to becoming a very wholesome and lovable person, if not, indeed, something of a saint

When all is said and done, however, the greater part of our laughter is still unexplained. Barring out the laugh malicious, or cruel or contemptuous, why do we laugh, most times ? Simply, I suppose, because the incongruous or ridiculous thing finds us glad to be alive. And if you want my belief about that, you can have it in two words. God understands !

There is sin and sorrow and suffering in the world enough and to spare, God knows, and plenty of times when we feel very unlike laughter. But life is not all sorrow and suffering. There are times when the sun is shining and happiness abounds, and health is splendid and life is brimming over. These days it is a benediction to meet a smiling face, " better than finding a five-pound note," " as if another candle had been lighted in the room." On a small pretext perhaps, one laughs because one feels like it. In spite of all the sorrow and the sadness always close at hand, one is vastly the better for it. And, as I said, I believe that God in His heaven hears and understands.

VII

SUPPOSING

THE Philippian jailer, "supposing that the prisoners had been fled," was just about to commit suicide when Paul assured him that they were all there. "How hasty!" we say, when we read the story. "Why did not the man wait till he had seen that his charges really had got away before he formed such a desperate resolve? There is no sense in meeting trouble half-way in that fashion." Quite so. But who is to throw the first stone at the Philippian jailer? We are all very good at supposing, and though it will not cure us of the habit, I fear, it may help a little if we deal frankly with ourselves in the matter of this failing.

First, then, let us realise that by our suppositions we often hurt *ourselves*. The hurt, as a matter of fact, is sometimes measurable by the family physician, for you can get into quite a distressing condition by merely supposing that you are ill, or are going to be ill!

When the poet Cowper was thirty-one years of

44

age he was appointed Reading Clerk in the House of Lords, a well-paid, comfortable office that might have kept him happily occupied all the rest of his days. But he threw it up just after he got it. And why? Because he thought he could not face a public assembly and listen to the sound of his own voice! He never tried. But he supposed he could not do it. That, of course, was enough, for if you suppose you wont be fit for a particular duty, then the chances are that you won't. If you suppose people are looking at you, you'll make them look. If you suppose you are a poor, weak creature whom nobody heeds, the world will clap just that very label upon you, and go on its cheerful way. The one unfailing consequence, whatever else may happen, is that you will hurt yourself, make yourself less useful, less happy than God meant you to be.

I often wonder why, when we are so fond of supposing, we don't suppose the happier possibilities. Somehow it is always the least comfortable possibility we lean to. The sudden telegram always means disaster, never good news. We do not, like the poet, " cleave ever to the sunnier side of doubt." And there is this at least to be said, that while the event is yet in the future, the " sunnier side " does one far less harm.

Secondly, let us realise that by our suppositions we often wrong *our friends*. We are constantly building up conclusions regarding the attitude of our friends, on the airiest of foundations. And, when we have heard the real explanation of some incident we did not understand, we have often had to feel ashamed of our miserable suppositions. Yet somehow our experiences never seem to teach us. Next week we worry as much as ever over our friend's cold little bow, supposing that he is offended, and forgetting to suppose that he may merely have a headache !

As we cannot know our brother's mind, neither can we know his circumstances. What may be a very easy victory over temptation for you, may be very hard for him. What he has to contend against might overcome you altogether. Yet when we weigh our friends in the balance, do we not always suppose their circumstances to be just as easy as our own ? For Christ's sake, let us try to be more charitable. Nobody but God can see into the heart, and so nobody but He can judge fairly. There is a fine and needful lesson in Lauchlan Maclean Watt's lines :—

> " Where have you been, my brother,
>   For I missed you from the street ?—
> I have been away, for a night and a day
>   On the Lord God's Judgment Seat.

And what did you find, my brother,
  When your judging there was done ?—
Weeds in my garden, dust in my doors,
  And my roses dead in the sun,

And the lesson I brought back with me,
  Like Silence, from above,
That upon God's throne there is room alone
  For the Lord whose heart is Love."

And, finally, by our suppositions we often wrong our *Father in heaven*. To suffer from a misfortune that has not yet arrived is to wrong Him, for what worthy son suspects that his father means him a hurt every time he does not exactly understand his purpose ? Though we call God our Father, how seldom we give Him that kind of trust ! Yet how many times has His loving kindness disappointed our fears !

There are some who keep records of the weather, and some who note down every penny they spend ; but there is another sort of diary which it would be a means of grace to many of us to keep, even for a short time—the record, namely, of each occasion when we supposed that some evil was to befall us or ours, and it never happened. In a year that would be a fair-sized volume, and the writing of it might make us humbler, and more trustful, and so, better Christian men and women.

How well did Samuel Rutherford remind one of his depressed correspondents that " our appre-

hensions are not canonical," are not, that is to say,
inspired by God. We make them ourselves.
What He would have us believe is that all things
work together for good to them that love God.
That is canonical. We have a divine warrant
for believing that.

" Manners," says Emerson very neatly, " are
just the happy way of doing things." I think
we might define faith in God in almost the same
terms. It is just the happy way of looking at
things. Let us all try to learn that better way

"*Gather up the fragments
that remain, that nothing be
lost.*"

(JOHN vi. 12.)

VIII

BY-PRODUCTS

WHEN the multitude had been served at the feast
which Jesus created out of a few small loaves and
fishes, He asked His disciples to " gather up the
fragments that remain, that nothing be lost."
It was an unexpected order. For one might have
thought that He who could create food for such
a number of people had no need to be concerned
about the fragments that were left. But that is
just the point. It is this very open-handed Christ
who is so desirous that there should be no waste.
It is the Creator of the Feast who asks that the
fragments be made use of. He wants nothing
lost, nothing at all, even where there is plenty.

Now this is something that our age is just
beginning to learn, the wisdom of caring for the
fragments. In the sphere of industry and practical science, this principle is being applied
with results that are simply wonderful. One of
the outstanding features in modern commercial
methods is summed up in the magic word " by-
products." It is like a romance to read about

D

what is done now with such rubbish of the manu-
factures as coal-tar, cotton-waste, old rags, and
scrap iron—all worthless things until men saw
that it would pay to gather up the fragments.
To-day we find a very marked tendency to turn
the slag-heap to some useful purpose. It has
been found to be well worth while.

But it is only in the business and industrial
world that we have, as yet, wakened up seriously
and generally to recognise that " useless " is a
word to be very cautiously spoken. Socially,
we have our slag-heaps still. Morally and spiritually, we have the classes that are useless, as we
think, to either God or man—the hooligan, the
jail-bird, the drunkard, the waster. At present
we brand them as hopeless and clap them in
prison, which is as if we flung them on the rubbish
heap. Ought it not to occur to us that these
bodies and minds and souls of men that make up
the slag-heap of society might also, if treated
scientifically, with the science that we learn from
Jesus, yield equally wonderful results ? Human
nature, after all, however hopeless it may seem,
is surely as susceptible of being turned to sound
civic and divine use as the waste of our factories.
" We get brilliant colours from the residual products of the gasworks. Can't we get something
as good," asks J. Brierley, " from the rubbish

heap of society ? " The thing is surely worth trying, seriously and hopefully.

It is being done, of course, by a small section of workers in the community ; for the home missionary and the workers in slums and Homes and Shelters are doing just what has been found so much worth while in the realm of daily business —they are utilising these by-products of civilisation for the glory of God and the good of society at large. But they could do far more if they got more help, more sympathy, and—quite frankly —more money. Business men of to-day believe thoroughly in the chemist who transforms the despised rubbish of the factory into things of use and even of beauty. Let them have as much faith in the social worker, the evangelist, the missionary, for they are doing the same kind of work. Let them show their faith and their approval as openly.

Christ's care for the fragments that men would disregard is in line with God's own unfailing practice. In the great factory of Nature there are no waste products, because all are turned to some further use. The dead leaves of last autumn go to make the soil of the spring. " The little streams that have watered the greenness of many meadows, go afterwards to do duty in the great sea. The vast surrounding atmosphere is made efficient over and over again for the breath of living men," and so on through countless instances.

And what God does in Nature, that He does in Grace. When Harold Begbie wrote his book about some typical cases of men and women whom the Salvation Army had rescued from dreadful shame and hopelessness, he called it, very appropriately, " Broken Earthenware." With a wise and loving patience the Army gathered these fragments together, and the book tells how God's grace made useful and honoured citizens of them.

And that suggests a question. If the ideal towards which man is working be—no slag-heaps, no waste - bings at all, but everything having any capacity it possesses hammered or rolled or boiled or chemically extracted out of it—may not that be God's Ideal too, the End towards which He is working, though He does not tell us yet, lest our knowledge should defeat His purpose ? There are men who think so, who hope so, though they can do no more. Tennyson, in a noble passage in " In Memoriam," expresses the hope which many feel :—

> " That nothing walks with aimless feet ;
> That not one life shall be destroy'd
> Or cast as rubbish to the void,
> When God hath made the pile complete."

In the light of our Lord's words in the Evangel, it is surely not an unworthy hope to hold. Shall God Himself, when His saints have gone singing into light at last, shall God Himself not pitifully gather up the fragments of mankind and make something even of them? Shall man as he grows in the knowledge which God gives, find more and more use for *his* waste, and a pile of useless lives lie for ever outside of *God's* Door?—lives which even Love can make nothing of, lives that are only fit to be cast away?

We may ask, but no man can answer. What we do know, however, is that " Now is the accepted time, now is the day of salvation."

As thy servant was busy here and there, he was gone."
(I KINGS xx. 40.)

IX

BUSY HERE AND THERE

A PROPHET once told the King a story, for purposes of his own, to the effect that, in a battle, an officer committed a captive to his charge and ordered him to guard him with his life. So he did for a while. But as the tide of battle came his way, he thought he could do more by lending a hand with his sword. So he sped into the press and laid about him lustily—and came back to find his captive vanished. " As thy servant was busy here and there, he was gone ! " " Served you right," said the King, in effect. And the King said true. Applied to the battle of life, it is still true.

We may learn from this parable, first, how opportunity is lost. We lose our chances, not because, as some of us complain, we never get them, but because when they come, we are somewhere else where we have no particular call to be. You miss seeing your friend because when his train starts you are not there. You miss an order because you were out golfing when the

customer called.   How many men have regretted
all their lives that they wrote their letter a day
late, that they put off their visit till the morrow !

Now, just as we get chances to succeed or better
ourselves in a material sense, so God is also, and
often at the very same time and by these very
channels, giving us chances to become better men
and women, to learn His will, to receive His
blessing.   And we miss these, as we miss the
others, because when the Spirit of God would deal
with ours, we are busy here and there, and the
chance is gone.

It may be that God has a message of peace to
breathe into your heart when, at the day's close,
you lay the day's work before Him and give Him
thanks and ask His forgiveness.   But when that
moment comes you are so interested in your book
that you tumble into bed unmindful, and the
Divine Spirit, with His message of peace, slips
away.

A week ago, or a month, it may be, God had
a tryst to meet you in His House, and a message
to give you.   But when the hour came and the
bells rang, you were not there—you best know
why.   That is how opportunity is lost.

We learn, also, from this story, that neglect
of the duty that lies at hand cannot be made
up for in any other way.   Maybe this prophet

fought bravely. Perhaps he accounted for a goodly number of the enemy himself. But that did not alter the fact that he did not guard his captive, which was the thing he was required to do.

Mrs Jellyby goes here and there, speaking at meetings, and conducts an enormous correspondence in the interest of her mission. And it is all very strenuous and impressive. But she will get no credit for it, and she deserves none. For in the home dwell her family of neglected children who do not know what the word " mother " means. If you engage some tradesman to work for you, and he scamps or neglects his duties, is it any consolation to you to learn that he practises assiduously on the violin every spare moment ? If God has laid some duty right in our path, and we avoid it, or do it perfunctorily, can we make up to Him for it, by doing something more agreeable with all our heart and soul ?

Thirdly, we learn from this story what we may call the divine order in our duties. Since I can only do one thing at a time, which am I to do at any given time, which am I to do first ? There is a right and a wrong order, of course, and our story shows us clearly which is which. FIRST, THAT WHICH IS NEAREST. There was no question of that in the prophet's case. It was to guard his captive. And there is seldom any serious question in our own case.

Behold, here is a mote in my brother's eye; is it not my nearest duty to take it out ? Nay, my brother, do you not rather mean that that is the more agreeable duty ? When you call it nearest, you confuse things that differ. Your nearest duty is to take the beam out of your own eye.

I would pay my vow to God, says one, and lay my offering upon His altar. Is not that my nearest duty ? Not for you, perhaps the Christ shall say. There may be something nearer still. First go and be reconciled to your brother, and then make your offering to God.

Here is life before me, says another, offering me rich rewards if I go in with courage and patience to possess it. Is it not my clear duty to bid for success, to make my fortune, to do well in my profession ? Nay, but even before that, if we will hear Jesus, there is something. " Seek ye *first* the Kingdom of God." Let us give that supreme place, lest haply, putting the others first, we find that while we are busy here and there, it has gone.

*" O Lord, revive Thy work in
the midst of the years."*
(Habakkuk iii. 2.)

X

" TOO OLD AT FORTY "

" Too old at forty " is a popular cry in these days,
and a somewhat pitiful one. For surely it is
only for the rank materialist that the best is past
when these bodily machines of ours have run
for forty years ? For the man whose life is in
touch with God's, it is not so. God never grows
old. And whoso of any of the sons of men opens
his life to the influence of that Eternal Life of
His, takes on something of its power to defy the
years. A man, says medical science, is as old
as his arteries. A man, says religion—and here
is the higher truth—is as old as his spirit. A spirit
revived in the midst of the years—that is religion's great offset to the fact that the fortieth
milestone lies behind one. The prescription for
perpetual youth is the life of faith. Believe in
God, ally yourself with Him, accept the thought
and gift of God which Jesus brings, and there is
nothing good, nothing really worth having,
nothing that God meant you to possess and to be

58

that is impossible for you yet, old in years though
you be.

We speak of Opportunity coming but once.
According to the formula I have just referred to,
it would seem to come only before forty. But
there is a great and hopeful Word of God that
challenges that formula and dares to call it false.
In its breadth and fulness the Gospel means the
gift of a fresh hope and the possibility of revival
even " in the midst of the years." You have
your chance yet, my brother. It is not too late.
The permanent and abiding riches of life are still
within your reach. I say its " permanent and
abiding riches." I have no authority to promise
you the lesser gifts. No amount of reviving, for
example, will ever enable fifty years of age to
play a hard game of football again, or climb a
difficult mountain. But, for my part, I am re-
luctant to believe that God means these feats
to be the ultimate glory of manhood.

Yet even here, one may say in passing, much
more is possible than one would think. The
bodily machine is wonderfully adaptable, even
when youth has gone. Physical salvation is even
then not an absolute impossibility. I saw a list,
recently, of the ages of those who reported themselves restored to bodily health by the course of
a well-known physical-culture expert, and there

were some sixty, and some threescore and
ten !

But, at least, the way is still open to life's
better gifts. If Opportunity be allowed to speak
for herself, this is what she says :—

> " They do me wrong who say I come no more,
>   When once I call and fail to find you in ;
> For, every day I stand outside your door,
>   And bid you wake and rise, to fight and win."

What is it you desire in the midst of the years ?
Name it to yourself, and if it be among the true
and abiding goods of life, God's word to you is
that you may have it yet.

It is commonly supposed that one is too old
after forty to begin mental culture or take an
interest in new ideas. But Robert Hall was over
sixty when he began to learn Italian that he
might read Dante. Arnold of Rugby commenced
Sanskrit just two years before his death. The
" Comment of Bagshot " on Morley's three-
volume Life of Gladstone is as follows : " If you
are feeling old, and are oppressed with the sense
that the future is little to you, go to this book
and see where Gladstone was at your age. Yesterday I was forty-nine, and all day long I
struggled with the thought that the fiftieth year
was the beginning of the end. It comforted me

amazingly to find that at this age Gladstone had
not yet got into his second volume."

Can you believe that God gave any man the
gift of life, meaning the first half of it to be the
best ? Can you believe that it is His purpose
that the most hopeless part of life should be its
end ? There are, it is true, certain faculties and
links with the material world that men shed as
they grow older. But these are of the husk of
life, and not of its kernel. Maturity of mind is
a greater thing than maturity of body, and comes
later. Maturity of soul, the greatest thing of all,
does not seem to come here at all. Souls are still
growing when they leave this lower School.
That is surely not " going down-hill." That is
what God means life to be for all of us, a road
that leads " uphill all the way." You have
seen a creeper growing up a high house wall. At
the top was a wealth of leaves and blossom,
spreading wider the higher it went. But, down-
wards, it all narrowed to a bare, wrinkled, single
stem, so touched by the passing seasons that,
but for the life above it, you would say it was
dead. So do the lower powers wither as time
goes on, but at the top there may be a life which
reaches ever upwards and broadens more and
more unto the perfect day.

When I think of what age may be and should

be, it is not to the world's cheerless maxim I
would turn, but rather to those well-known lines
of Browning, who, here as elsewhere, so nobly
interprets for us the Christian hope :—

> " Grow old along with me,
>   The best is yet to be,
> The last of life, for which the first was made.
>   Our times are in His Hand
>   Who saith, 'A whole I planned ';
> Youth shows but half : trust God : see all : nor be afraid."

Too old at forty ? Too old for what ? Not
too old to be past reviving with all that God's
revival means. Not too old to begin even yet
the life God meant to be. There is an opportunity for all that still, for—

> " Every day is a fresh beginning,
> Every morn is the world made new.
>   You who are weary of sorrow and sinning,
> Here is a beautiful hope for you,
> A hope for me and a hope for you.

> All the past things are past and over,
> The tasks are done, and the tears are shed,
>   Yesterday's errors let yesterday cover,
> Yesterday's wounds, which smarted and bled,
> Are healed with the healing which night has shed.

> Let them go since we cannot relieve them,
>   Cannot undo, and cannot atone.
> God, in His Mercy, receive, forgive them.
>   To-day is ours and to-day alone.

> Every day is a fresh beginning.
> Listen, my soul, to the glad refrain ;
>   And, spite of old sorrow and older sinning,
> And puzzles forecasted and possible pain,
> Take heart with the day and begin again."

For revival is God's most willing gift, even " in the midst of the years."

XI

TWO-TALENT PEOPLE

THE man in the parable who received two talents
suffers somewhat from his place in the story,
because he stands, where he is apt to be over-
looked, between a conspicuous success and a
very dramatic failure. Yet of the three he is
the character that best deserves our attention,
for he is the average man. He is the brother—
if I dare say so—of us all. He belongs to our
own family of the two-talented, the largest family
in the world. Possibly we did not always admit
that it is he who is our brother, for it is the
glorious prerogative of youth to believe that its
true sphere is among those who do great things.
But the years put most of us quietly in our place ;
we grow into the discovery that, after all, we are
just ordinary. Since it is a critical time in a
man's life when his limitations are brought home
to him, I like to think that it was to safeguard
us against the perils of that discovery that Jesus
brought an ordinary average person into His

64

story, and showed that he too might earn his " Well done."

We all know that the five-talent man has his special temptations. Miss Julia Wedgwood, in her " Nineteenth Century Teachers," has a chapter on " The Vanity of the Great Men of Letters." Vanity, then, let us say, is the besetting sin of the greatly gifted. And the parable itself shows us what the very poorly endowed is too apt to do—nothing at all, because there is so little he can do. But the average man has his peculiar temptations also. One of them is envy. Don't we all believe that if we had our friend's abilities we could do something really worth while ? Don't we sometimes say that, if we had the chances that some have, we could do better ? The cure for this trouble is to read the parable of the Talents, keeping our eye specially on the man with two. He only added other two, we are told. That is not a very brilliant result. But I ask you to notice that Christ declares that he filled his niche as perfectly in God's scheme of things as even the five-talent man did. You will not find a syllable of difference in the welcome accorded to him at the last. The average man did what he could ; and the brilliant man did no more. It is a waste of time, therefore, for the two-talent people to envy those

E

with five, for " the blessed work of helping the
world forward," as George Eliot says, " does not
wait to be done by perfect men."

A much commoner fault of the average man's
than envy, however, is that he continually under-
estimates his power His power ? says some
one. What power has a two-talent man compared with one who has five ? The answer is :
Six times five are thirty, but fifty times two are
a hundred. That is not nonsense. The power
of the two-talented is the power of littles to add
up into huge totals. The strength of the average
man lies in combination. He counts because
there are so many of him.

It is the average, ordinary people who do by
far the biggest share of the world's work, and of
God's work in the world. If the cottages and the
ordinary-sized houses forbear to sweep before
their own doors, not all the five-acre fronts in
the town will keep it clean. We ordinary people
may never head a reformation or do anything
remarkable. That we admit very heartily. But
we forget that, by joining up all our efforts, we
can do more for any cause of God or man than
all the reformers of history taken together.

But, besides his temptations, the ordinary
person has his advantages. In Lord Kelvin's
" Life " it is said, of a certain mathematical

article which he published, that there were just one or two other men in the world capable of appreciating it. It must be a lonely thing to be a five-talent man !

It is to the two-talent man that the higher honour belongs of playing his part in obscurity. He has no audience to cheer him on. He must do his duty without any reporter to chronicle his deed. Where the five-talent people are, audience and reporter are never far away. But the hard thing is to be brave with no one to encourage, to be loyal to Christ and duty in a sphere that is never observed—and that is the privilege of ordinary people only. The men and women of no account have to do their work without recognition—and they are doing it every day. Who is there to see or to tell of the sacrifices that are made constantly and cheerfully in humble homes ? There are deeds of pure moral courage done in the world of business quite fit to compare with those which on a battlefield earn the Victoria Cross. It would be foolish, of course, to say that any class has a monopoly of heroism, but if you want to find it of the purest and the finest you must look for it among those who have fewest incentives and encouragements—

"The bravely dumb that did their deed,
And scorned to blot it with a name."

There remains this further glorification of
the average man that he has his place, secure
and inspiring, in the remembrance and the trust
of Christ. Why do you think Jesus put this
two-talent man into the story at all ? There
was no need for it. The story is complete without him. The lesson is sufficiently plain if you
consider the five-talent man on the one hand
and the one-talent man on the other. Yes, but
in that way the common people would have
been forgotten : the average man who knew
that he had not five talents to work with would
have read this story and gone away sorrowful
because it was not for him. So, out of His knowledge and feeling for ordinary souls, Jesus told
how one who had only received two talents
gained two other talents beside them, and He
forgot not to add that to him also his master said,
" Well done, thou good and faithful servant."
This is our Lord's recognition of ordinary people.
It is His gracious acceptance of commonplace
service. It is the charter and beatitude of those
who can only do a little. Blessed are they, in
our Master's eyes, who DO THAT LITTLE, for they
also shall have their " Well done " at the last.

XII

THE MIRAGE AND THE POOL

A THIRSTY traveller on the hot sands sometimes sees before him a level stretch of water, promising him coolness and refreshment. But as he journeys towards this oasis, it recedes farther and farther away ; and he may die of thirst, with the means of assuaging it, to all appearance, within easy reach. For the thing he sees is a mirage. Mirage, therefore, is another name for a cruel disappointment, a vision that mocks by its unreality. So that when the Prophet Isaiah declares in God's name that one day the " mirage shall become a pool," he is telling very good news indeed. He means that our visions of the coming good shall solidify at last, that what we think we see afar off shall yet exist, that we dream of good which we shall come up to some day.

Well, there are many earnest souls dreaming of good to-day, seeing visions of the cities of earth transformed into actual cities of God, with streets clean and safe, with no poor sempstress dying of starvation in her garret but a stone's-throw from

69

the dwellings of the rich, with no stunted children, blasted by drink and vice, scrambling about miserably in the gutters—visions of the time when the land shall be inhabited and yield its increase, when the brotherhood and love for men which those of Christ's name and Church profess, shall gird itself and serve, and not allow an honest, willing workman to come to want, nor one single child to be cheated of its birthright of sunshine and health and happiness. Men are seeing such visions to-day. We thankfully acknowledge that not a little has been done to realise them. But beyond all our poor progress, this fairer picture of what might be gleams and glimmers ahead of us. "A mirage," say the critics, "a thing in the air, beautiful, but not solid nor practical."

But a mirage, mark you, is not a mere hallucination. It is, the physicist tells us, actually an IMAGE OF SOMETHING EXISTING, not where it seems to be, but somewhere else farther away. I want you to note that carefully. The thing seen does not exist where it appears, because the path by which the rays have travelled is a bent one, and the eye is deceived, BUT IT DOES EXIST SOMEWHERE—it may be miles farther on.

Now, when you call the social reformer's dream a mere mirage, do you see what you have said ?

A mirage is a vision, with reality behind it and explaining it. That we are seeing pictures to-day of a cleaner social life, of cities without slums, of parishes without poorhouses, and streets of children getting a chance to grow as God meant them, is not a meaningless circumstance. Men may say it is a mirage, if they please. But, if so, then the reality itself lies somewhere in God's keeping, on in front, and we shall come to it if we " work hard, pray hard, and hope eternally."

You need to be reminded, also, that YOUR mirage shall become a pool. For there is a disappointment that attends the pursuits of any high ideal. You step out the years that ought to have brought you to the place, and the thing is not there yet. Temptations, whose power seemed spent, have risen up afresh to hinder you. Temper perhaps is dying hard. The Christlike in character sometimes seems as far away as ever. " I've seen myself afar off," a man says, " the Christ-follower I should like to be, but as I move forward the vision recedes before me. My ideal is, after all, a mirage, an intangible, impossible thing, and I sometimes ask myself whether it is worth while to go on."

Ah, my brother, you'll go on, I think, whatever happens. For yours is the vision which, once seen, " poisons all meaner choice for ever-more." In Madagascar they have a quaint custom which ordains that when a prisoner sees the queen and salutes her he goes free, no matter what his crime may be. So do men who have once looked upon the Ideal in the face of Jesus find an immediate liberty and a horizon without bounds. The old " uninterrupted view across the street " satisfies them no more.

But there are ways of following. And of all the means by which earnest men have sought to persuade their fellows into travelling hopefully after the vision they have seen, this of Isaiah's, for sheer optimism and daring, is chief. He does not blink the fact of the mirage, its mockery, and its disappointment. He does not say you won't be cheated again. But he declares your IDEAL EXISTS SOMEWHERE, and you will come to it, if you go on.

That is what you ought to believe. What you see of yourself, at your best and highest—that is God's thought of you, reaching you, like the ray of the mirage, from somewhere out of sight. As the father saw the prodigal a great way off, and said, even then, in his heart, " It is my son," so has the Father in His heart, even now, your full, true image and stature, as you will be when you have attained. In the mirage-like ideal that plays before you sometimes, He is letting you catch a glimpse of your own true picture. Isn't it a splendid thought, and worth believing ?—that your ideal of yourself is a faint shadow of the full, perfect picture of you which, fatherlike, God cherishes even now in His heart ?

" Would he not be a mere fool," says an old writer, quoted by Dr W. M. Macgregor, " who, running at a tournament with others, and falling in the best of his career, should lie weeping on the ground and afflicting himself with discourses on his falling ? Man, they would tell him, lose no time ; get up and take the course again, for he that rises quickly and continues his race, is as if he had never fallen."

Up, then, my brother, and take the road again after your vision. " Pray hard, work hard, and hope eternally," with God's promise singing in your heart, for YOUR mirage shall yet become a pool !

XIII

THE DUTY OF PRAISING PEOPLE

I WONDER if there is anyone who has not felt better, and felt it in him to try to do better, just because of some kindly encouragement received from a friend ? Even the lower animals respond to such treatment. Your dog will wag his tail in a frenzy of delight if he thinks he has pleased you. It is an easy thing to work exceedingly hard in an atmosphere of appreciation, just as it is a trial to do even a simple thing in the sight of those who are critical and censorious.

We have all found it so, I take it. Well, then, why should we not do as we like to be done by ? Why should not we make a point of encouraging our friends in this way, when we get a chance ? In other words, isn't there really a DUTY of praising people, when they deserve it or need it ? If you think a man is facing well up to a difficult situation, tell him so. If he is turning out a good article in his business, tell him so. If your wife has excelled herself with a cake or pudding, tell her so. If your friend's son has been successful

at College, let the father know that you have
heard of it. We Scotch people have really an
excessive gift of silence. We may be as proud
as Lucifer over the achievement of some relative
or friend, but it takes a very great deal of pressure
to get us to say so ; and even then, as likely as
not, we mix some bitter with the sweet, for health's
sake ! After all, it is hardly encouraging for the
person who has done his best for you, to hear the
result characterised as " Not bad." It is certainly not excessive laudation to say of something
that some one at home has done, and done really
well, that " It might be worse ! " Yet these are
just the stones that we sometimes offer to our
best beloved for bread. Doubtless they understand. But, now and again, they must be chilled
and discouraged.

Of course, what we are afraid of is that we
shall minister to our friend's pride and make
him conceited. But though " swelled head " is
certainly a very irritating complaint, I don't
think it is nearly so common as we suppose. We
judge in this matter far too much by outward
appearances, which are very often deceptive.
To my mind, there is something far more common, and just as hurtful,—self-depreciation, dis-
couragement, self-distrust. There are men doing
their level best, and near to breaking down and

giving up their attempt, whom a little encouragement would revive, as water does a plant. There are women slaving and toiling away in many a busy home, and the last straw of their burden often is that they get no word of thanks for it. Nobody notices, and nobody seems to care.

Now I am prepared to assert that it is worth while risking any harmful effects if, by a timely, kindly encouragement, one can revive hope in the depressed and discouraged, or lift a life in spirit above an uncongenial environment, or fan the embers of some worthy ambition which else had gone out in darkness. Such things praise, sincerely given, can do and has many a time done. I say it is worth the risk. And the risk after all is slight. For, as J. M. Barrie has said, " The praise that comes of love does not make us vain, but humble rather."

In a magazine recently I saw a distinction drawn between what were called " plus " and " minus " people. Did you ever think that there are people whose most fitting symbol is a " minus " sign ? They never add to your happiness or your hopes or your faith either in your self or anybody else. Rather they take away from these. When they leave your company, you feel that you are somehow poorer than you were, in your own esteem, and in your belief in others.

These are the "minus" people. But there are others, thank God, of a different sort. They never come to us, but they add to our store of all the best things far beyond their thought or intention. They believe in us, and so help us to do better. They draw out the best side of us, and sometimes that side surprises even ourselves. They radiate courage and hope and faith. Their praise humbles us, yet leaves us tingling with desire to be more worthy of it. I ask you, Is it not better to be "plus" than "minus"?

"You remember," says James Lane Allen in "The Choir Invisible," "the woman who broke the alabaster box for the feet of our Saviour while He was living—that most beautiful of all the appreciations? And you know what we do—let our fellows carry their crosses to their calvaries, and, after each has suffered his agony and entered into his peace, we go out to him and break our alabaster boxes above his stiff, cold feet. I have always hoped that my religion might enable me to break my casket for the living who alone can need it—and who always do need it."

Beautiful — and true. Here and now is the time to let our esteem and our knowledge of our friends' worth peep out occasionally in speech or action, here and now, in the burden and heat of the day, when the most hopeful are sometimes discouraged, and the strongest sometimes faint. It will do us no harm. And, who knows ? but it may be reckoned by them, in its timeliness and helpfulness as among the tender mercies of God.

" The street shall be built
again, and the wall, even in
troublous times."

(DANIEL ix. 25.)

XIV

BUILDING IN TROUBLOUS TIMES

THE early legends of mankind tell us of fabled
cities that were built to music. But nothing is
built that way nowadays; and the prophet for
us is the man who neither blinks nor minimises
the dust and din of actual life, and yet has the
faith to declare, as Daniel does, that " the wall
shall be built even in troublous times," that it
is out of that very turmoil that the City of God
we hope for is going to come. Daniel's, therefore, is a message for us still, reminding us that
it is not to music that we build for God in these
days, but amid a din and confusion that hide from
us often what is really happening. It is in the
stress of the times that the walls of God's purpose in the world are being builded stone by
stone.

Let us look at some of our trouble centres in
the light of this brave faith. There is, for example,
the present social and industrial unrest. Everyone knows what that means. In almost every
branch of industry there are restlessness, discontent,

grievances. Strikes are becoming more and more frequent and serious. It is difficult even for those who are in sympathy with a sane democratic ideal, as the Church of Christ, of all institutions, ought to be, to predict what is to happen, or to approve of everything that is said and done in the name of liberty. It is a troublous time, in very truth, an anxious time, a time of stress and clamour, and apparently nothing more.

But there is something more. It is too soon yet to see it, because of the confusion; but as sure as there is a hand of God moving in history, out of this trouble is coming, and shall come, some solid piece of enduring building. A more stable social fabric is coming. Greater content and happiness and justice all round—these are coming. And the time—

" When man to man the world ower
Shall brothers be, for a' that "

—that is coming, out of all this upturn and re-volution. It is a law of God. First the thunder-storm, and then the clear, cool air. First the struggle of which evolutionists tell us, and then the emergence of the more perfect animal. There is no reform we enjoy to-day but was born out of agitations, often extreme and over-zealous. For it is not in the dead, dull, uneventful days so

much as in the very stress and strain of the times
that the wall of social progress is built.

Another of our troubles to-day is the general
unsettlement of religious beliefs. Ours, whatever it be, is not an age of serene and simple faith.
Its coat-of-arms, some one has said, is a " Bishop
dormant, and a point of interrogation rampant,
and the motto ' Query.' " Within our generation
the Universe has become suddenly roomier and
more wonderful. A vast inrush of knowledge,
hidden from our fathers, has lifted us, as on some
tide, to other points of view whence the outlook
is strange and unfamiliar. And the consequence
meantime is that many loyal souls are troubled.
The fearful are crying, " Turn back to the simpler
ways and thoughts of our fathers ! " But it
can't be done. There is no turning back, there
is no looking back even, in the Kingdom of God.
The way is forward, and only forward, in loyalty
to His leading.

For indeed there is nothing to fear. Out of
this unsettlement the wall is being built. Out
of this confusion is coming, has come in some
degree already, a stronger, broader, larger faith
which will have room in its arms for every truth
that patience and genius can gather in the many-
volumed library of God. This very age which
is so unsettled doctrinally is more incurably

F

religious in desire and longing than ever before. When the Commission on Coast Erosion visited the Isle of Wight, they found that while the sea had encroached on one part of the shore, there had been an extension of the coast on another part by fresh deposits ; and I am perfectly certain that that is what is happening at present in the realm of faith and doctrine. Behind all its pulling down, this age is building up more nobly and enduringly than before, and when the dust clears away we shall see that it is so. Because, it is out of the shaking—and remember it is God Himself who of set purpose shakes the world and men's thoughts—it is out of the shaking that the truth comes that cannot be shaken, and so abides.

There are also the trouble-centres of our daily living. Not for any of us is life a very simple or soft thing. All of us, professional and business men, heads of families, mothers and housewives cumbered with monotony and much service, all of us are in the stress of things one way or other and need some strong, sure word of comfort at times to send us back hopefully to our tasks.

Such a word is here. Brethren, busy, burdened, tempted, there is more going on in your life than you can see. You think at times that you are merely ploughing the sands ? I tell you No, you are building also, you are building a Christian character in the only way in which it can be built, by conflict, through trial, and in the face of temptation. Out of the strain and the dust is coming to you, though you cannot see it, something more of strength and patience. You are growing, as the motto of one of the Covenanters on the Bass had it, you are growing under your load.

The chrysalis works and struggles out of its mummy-like swathings, and emerges from the conflict a creature much higher up the scale, a perfect insect with wings and legs. That is what your struggles and conflicts are doing for you. They are lifting you up in the scale of manhood, and bringing you nearer to God. It is not in the barracks that soldiers are made. It is not in the harbour that the ship finds itself, but out upon the troubled and banging seas. And it is in the thick and stress of life that character is built up within us. It is by following the Christ, not in thought in the cloister, but along the actual, hard, and toilsome ways of daily duty, that some enduring likeness to Him is stamped upon our lives.

" You train your powers, and the training is arduous, but the reward is more life. You keep your temper amid the daily distractions of office and warehouse, and there is built up in you, out of that discipline, a larger self-restraint. You fight your temptations like a Christian, and out of the conflict comes a greater power to withstand. You do your duties loyally, and as they pass they leave you, for a heritage, the ability to do bigger duties." Amid all your striving, something great and real is going on. The times may be very troublous, but the wall is being built.

Perhaps, in all this, it has seemed as if the most that one could say of the discipline of life is to counsel the faith that, somehow or other, it is building up a soul within us. Ah, but there is more than that. When Daniel's friends were in the furnace, you remember, there walked with them one who was like unto the Son of God. Don't let us forget that. In the very straitest of the times there is One with us also, to help and befriend.

> "We fight, but 'tis He who nerves our arm,
> He turns the arrows that else might harm,
> And out of the storm He brings a calm.
> And the work that we count so hard to do,
> He makes it easy, for He works too."

" The length and the breadth
and the height of it are equal."
REVELATION xxi. 16.)

XV

CHARACTER, IN THREE DIMENSIONS

ST JOHN observed of the City of God which he saw in his vision, that the length and breadth and height of it were equal. I wish to suggest to you that the character of its citizens should conform to the same measurements. That should be equal in its length, breadth, and height.

Let us try to make this clear to ourselves. First, as to LENGTH. The meaning here is best suggested if you think of the word " line." We speak of a man having a " line," the thing he does, the object of his chief interest, his business, craft, or profession, whatever it be. And what is the ideal here ? Why, send it out as far as you can. Follow your line. Put your heart into your business. Be ashamed of no labour and of no detail which will help you along your line.

It is a very common, and a false idea of the Christian religion to suppose that it has nothing to do with a matter like this. Believe me, it has. The man has got hold of religion by the wrong end somehow for whom it weakens interest in his daily business. There is a certain stage of piety to which men sometimes attain when they begin to apologise for being grocers, lawyers, and so forth. For my part I never could believe that the Master thought any more of them for that. He was once a Carpenter Himself. And it would shake my belief in Him very seriously if it should be proved that He was not a competent one, if, because He had something greater to do by and by, He never tried really to learn that craft.

Let your plans for the days to come be as earnest and as full of labour as you can make them. You are not one whit the less a Christian on that account. Plan for your self-development as generously as may be, and God bless you in all your endeavours. Follow your line !

Having set before ourselves the ideal of length, of self-culture, and development, we want very clearly to realise, in the second place, that by itself that is a very inadequate standard of Christian character. Not that I take back anything I have said. That all stands. But if it stand alone, it is of little worth.

We must bid for BREADTH of character to the same extent, and with the same earnestness. And that is by no means so easy or so common. Length, without breadth, is simply selfishness, pedantry, professionalism. There are people who seem to be interested only in their own line, impatient of those whose tastes differ, calmly contemptuous of everything to right and left of them. And the impression which they make is as disagreeable as it is un-Christian. You see the peril? Let our ideal be to avoid that. Along with length, bid for breadth!

The priest and the Levite in Christ's story both followed out their line exclusively, and stand pilloried for all time as types of selfishness, examples to be avoided. The Samaritan, who had breadth enough to let him cross the road and tend the wounded man, alone approaches the Christian ideal of character.

Spinoza has declared that " our rank in the scale of being is determined entirely by the objects in which we are interested." And our Lord Himself has made it very, very clear that he who is interested only in himself stands in the lowest rank of all. One-half of the law of God, according to Jesus, is that you " love your neighbour as yourself," take an interest in his affairs, put yourself in his place, sympathise with his line or his want of line.

That may cost you time and labour and other things. It may hamper you in your own line, in fact. But what you lose there you will gain in this other direction—breadth—and by so much will come nearer to the ideal symmetry of Christian character.

We can all say quickly enough what we are doing for ourselves. But there is another question which the spirit of the age is forcing into a new prominence—What are you doing for your neighbour?

You see, then, what it means to bid for breadth as well as length? It means that, for all our attempts at self-culture, we must try to keep an open mind towards lines of growth and interest and pleasure which may be far enough removed from our own. It means that we consecrate ourselves to that larger service of Christ which is service of all to whom we can be of any use. Busy as we try to be, let us resolve that we shall never be so busy that we are blind to our brother's sorrow or his joy. Let us beware of knowledge without charity. It is a good thing to be an expert, but it is better still, in addition, to be a friend.

Yet you may have length and breadth, and still come short of even rudimentary Christian character. For our life is not touched with the divine symmetry till, to these others, we have added HEIGHT, religion, devotion, faith, the uplift and response of the whole man to God.

Let your eye and your heart travel upwards to the "measure of the stature of the fulness ot Christ." That gives you height. Turn to the great Christian biographies, and note there the continual upward reference of the spirit to God, to Whom it belongs. That again is a height measurement. Or listen to some humble soul saying, in his darkness, " I will fear no evil for Thou art with me," and remember that he is speaking to God. That gives you height, once more.

The advice which Sir Deryck Brand in " The Rosary " gives to Jane Champion is : " Go to New York City, and see how, when a man wants a big building and has only a small plot of ground, he makes the most of that ground by running his building up to the sky. Learn to do likewise." Isn't it there that most of us come short ? Biologists tell us that the pineal gland is really the rudiment of an upward-looking eye, an eye on the top of the head. Some of us have to confess that there is another sense in which our upward-looking eye is a mere rudiment. Yet the direction upward is the most natural of all. It is the home road. For God made us for Himself.

There are ideas, as you know, which are being shaken and destroyed to-day by the advance of science. But there are others which, by that same agency, are being but more firmly established. And in this latter class are such pillar-facts as these : That nothing transforms character like fellowship with Jesus Christ ; that there is no truer help for daily living than the help which prayer brings down from God ; that no one is better fitted to meet the chances and changes of life than the man who has put his trust in God and committed all his ways to Him. And, my brethren, these are all measurements of height. What sort of a bid are we making for that direction ? Do we need to answer ? Does the best of us need to answer ? I think not. But that is not all. Listen :—

> " I came to the throne with a sin-stained soul ;
>   The old year was done.
> ' Dear Father, hast Thou a new leaf for me ?
>   I have spoiled this one.'
> He took the old leaf, stained and blotted,
> And gave me a new one, all unspotted,
>   And into my sad heart smiled,
>   ' Do better now, my child ! ' "

The ideal Christ-like character is threefold, and the last dimension is the most important, as well as the most neglected. So let us begin with that, with height. " Touch us," let us say to God our Father, " with a new sense that Thou desirest our fellowship, our service, and our love, and that we owe these to Thee. Bring us all nearer to

Thee, through Christ who is the Way." Also, remembering the need for breadth, let us ask Him to " help us to love our neighbour as ourselves." And, since length is needed too, let us add the prayer, " Give us to go blithely on our business every day."

XVI

THE PERIL OF THE EMPTY HEART

WHEN Jesus told how the evil spirit, finding the house, out of which it had been cast, swept and garnished but empty, returned with seven other devils more wicked than itself, He was showing the peril of the empty heart. He was teaching that the life that is empty, no matter how clean it may be, is a dangerous life.

Now we know that there is such a danger in Nature. She " abhors a vacuum," as the old philosophers said. If you leave your fields empty, she will fill them, if only with nettles and weeds. If you can't or won't fill a space with something useful, then Nature will fill it, though it be with rubbish.

And we know that there is this peril in human nature. Burton, in his " Anatomy of Melancholy," says that one great cause of this trouble is simply idleness. " The horse in the stable that never travels, the hawk in the mew that never flies, are both subject to diseases from which they might be free." And how, he asks, can an idle man

92

hope to escape? As a matter of fact, he does not. Who is so prone to imaginary ailments, who so full of whims and fancies, who such a nuisance to his neighbours as the man who has nothing to do, no occupation, no interest in life, no hobby even?

And in the spiritual life, as Jesus here declares, the peril is not less. It besets a man who has had his heart swept clean, even by the grace of God. He neither drinks nor smokes nor dances nor swears nor plays cards now. And he goes to the Kirk, or some other meeting. He is in dead earnest now. He is proud of his clean house, seeing others about him that are very different. This one drinks, that one swears, a third plays cards. And as he looks he forgets the great eternal law of brotherliness and love. He begins to feel that he is a child of God more than these, and he makes them feel it or he tells them so. He is degenerating into that pitiful thing, an unlovable Christian, whom even good men shun. When godliness has become uncharitable and censorious and self-righteous, the evil spirits from the wilderness have come back, and the last state of that man is worse than the first.

But the very emphasis which Jesus lays on the emptiness of the house suggests the cure. Fill the house, of course. As some old divine put it quaintly, " The devil himself can't fill your bag with beans, if you have filled it with peas ! " If you want to avoid the peril of the empty heart, keep your heart full of hopes, of ideals, of love for God and man. Cobwebs don't gather in corners that are dusted every day. Not all retired men are hypochondriacs. For, in place of their former occupation, they get some new one, though it be only gardening, fishing, or golf.

I came on the car the other day with a Salvation Army lass who had a large white button, pinned on her dress, bearing this motto, " Saved, to serve." If she carries out that ideal, she will steer wide of the peril of the empty heart. It is the men and women who are content to be saved and sit still all their lives after and talk about it, whose empty heart is a standing invitation to the first evil spirit passing that way.

For whether we speak of being saved or use some other form of words, whether we wear our motto on our buttonhole or in our heart, the fact remains that we begin the Christ-life for a purpose which is not exhausted as long as we are here. God saves no man that he may sit still. The Grace of God cleanses no man's heart that it may stand empty. We are " saved," as the Salvationist says, to serve. And if you look for your service and do it with all your strength, you will be tolerably safe at any rate from this danger.

It is nothing less than the whole round of Christian duty, nothing less than a complete response to the Spirit and Example of Christ in every aspect and corner of our lives, nothing less than that we accept when we start out on the Christian life. It embraces every human and Christian virtue, humility, charitableness, gentleness, long-suffering, helpfulness, sympathy, as well as faith, prayerfulness, and joy. And the long and the short of it is that the man who takes that for his ideal, or tries to take it, has his heart full. He has enough to satisfy him, and far more than he can practise. And that keeps him from the peril of the empty heart,—a full, wide Gospel, a Christ who is not a figure in a mechanical transaction, but a living, personal Saviour, Ideal and Teacher. The parable is His, and its warning is clear and stern. For the life to which He calls men is real and strenuous, and the wilderness where the evil spirits dwell is never very far off.

> " Does the road wind uphill all the way ?
>   Yes, to the very end.
>   Will the day's journey take the whole long day ?
>   From morn to night, my friend."

XVII

THE STORM AND THE VOICE

I WANT you to think for a little while of that
dramatic incident in Elijah's life when he watched
a storm in Horeb, and was unimpressed, and then,
in the after silence, heard a still small voice in his
heart which was for him the very Voice of God.
Wind, earthquake, and fire he had resisted.   But
that still small voice broke his heart.   The Lord,
he learned, was there, in that silence.

Some people, reading this incident, tell us it
means that the world of Nature has no message,
nothing that counts, for the spirit of man.   They
know not what they say, for instantly a score of
poets will start up to ask :

> "Not God ! in gardens ! when the eve is cool ?
> Nay, but I have a sign ;
> 'Tis very sure He walks in mine ! "

And we plain simple folk who are not poets know,
of a surety, that here and there and yonder in
the wide pleasance of Nature we have indeed been
brought very near to God.   There are hours that

shine like jewels in memory's store, when, as we stood upon some lonely hillside, or lay and listened to the sighing of the wind through the bent, or heard the long splash of the sea on a quiet night of stars, we found ourselves, of a sudden as it were, at the Gate Beautiful of the very Temple of the Most High, and bowed our spirits awhile in instinctive and willing worship. Let no one say that Nature has nothing for the spirit of man. Yet Nature's after all, is but a dumb helpfulness. That is what these people really mean to say. And that is the truth. Nature can but lay its hand upon us in a mute pity. It cannot speak. And it is a voice we need most when our hurt is sorest. What avails it to the man whose heart is breaking that the woods are green, and vocal with bird-music ? He will only ask, in his perplexity :—

> " Ye banks and braes o' bonnie Doon,
>   How can ye bloom sae fresh and fair ?
> How can ye chant, ye little birds,
>   And I sae weary, fu' o' care ? "

They do better, or so it seems to me, who read this dramatic parable in Horeb to mean that the quieter, stiller, gentler forces have more of God in them than those that are loud and terrifying, that they effect more, reach deeper, and endure longer. It was a tremendous storm that shook

G

Horeb, but it passed and left the prophet with head erect and pride unbroken.

Now, it is everywhere the mark of ignorance to lay stress on what is loud and noisy. The untaught observer explains a landscape by giant upheavals, mighty contending forces, earthquakes, and fire from heaven. But the wise man points rather to the silent, steady pressure of the ice, the constant erosion of running water, the slow silting of rivers, the action of frost and sun and wind and rain, century after century.

And one of the things hardest to learn is that just that very truth runs up into the spiritual realm, that God is working all about us in the quiet and gentle influences that move us to our decisions and touch our lives day by day as with fairy fingers, far more effectively than in the sudden catastrophes that draw men's eyes.

That, indeed, was just the lesson Elijah needed to learn, for his methods were much too turbulent and catastrophic. And he had made a distinct advance when he had learned that the still voice did a diviner work upon his own heart than all the uproar and riot of the great storm he watched.

Don't let us forget the prophet's lesson. In all our work for the causes of Christ and humanity, let us never forget that gentleness does more than rudeness, that a quiet word sinks deeper than a

loud appeal, that a hand upon the shoulder wins
when an upraised club only stiffens defiance.

Thank the Lord, we can be getting His work
successfully and lastingly done though we are
not making any noise about it. Campaigns
heralded with trumpets have their use in stirring
the indifferent, but nobody pretends that they
do anything like the amount of good accomplished
by quiet, persistent, regular ministration. In
so far as our generation is truly Christian we owe
it far more to the mothers in our homes than to
all the evangelists of our time put together, and
I have heard the best of them say so.

These are the days of fuss and bustle and
advertising. We are all for taking the world
by storm. That cause is called most prosperous
which is most talked about, and he is doing the
best work who is making the biggest splash. Ah
well, don't let that dishearten us, or tempt us
to be cynical. Quiet, patient loyalty, day after
day, counts for most in the end, as the coral insect
raises its island, cell by cell, out of the Pacific.
There is no better advertisement for Christ than
a sincere, humble, Christ-like life. The still small
voice of daily witness-bearing touches hearts
that gusty methods and violent efforts only move
to a more stubborn refusal. Niagara makes a
vast noise, and is a great sight to see ; but it is

not the Niagaras that keep the land green and fruitful. That is the obscure work of thousands of little nameless streams that flow softly.

Best and wisest interpreters of all, I think, are those who learn, from this vivid passage of Scripture and a man's experience, that the divinest thing in life, as we know it, is a still small Voice. But it took the world a long time to come to this. We read, in the sacred records of Israel, of a Mount on which the living God drew near to men. Thunder-clouds wreathed its top, and shot their bolts down its sides. It was smoking hot with God's presence, so that no one dared approach it. As we look upon that old-world picture of the majesty and awful aloofness of God, we feel the same awe in us that fell upon that people. But our hearts do not open to Sinai's thunders. The Lord is not there for us. Diviner far than Sinai for us is a hill called Calvary, where Jesus of Nazareth gave His life for men. More God-like than the impersonal mutterings of Israel's inaccessible mountain is Christ's " Come unto me all ye that labour and are heavy laden," or His " Father, forgive them, for they know not what they do." There is the Voice at last. Men who have braved the terrors of the Law have bowed their heads at the sound of that Voice and yielded themselves there in surrender to the Highest, seeking no other God than Him.

And it has not ceased. That Voice is speaking still to-day in the hearts of all who love Him. That is the wonderful fact. We read Shakespeare and Milton, but we do not hear them. We do not read Christ at all. He speaks to us, an inward voice, or else we do not know Him. Religion is just hearing that voice. Life at its noblest is just following it. Once a man has felt the Spirit of Christ dealing with him alone, not as a teacher from without, but as a Voice from within, he has found the shrine that can never be rifled, the chamber of peace that can never be invaded. Creeds may alter, forms of worship change, new views emerge. These things do not harm him, for he does not ground his faith on these. His divinest thing, his most sacred possession is the Christ whom he meets, and the quiet Voice which he sometimes hears, in his own heart. And so he can declare :—

> " Loud mockers in the roaring street
>   Say ' Christ is crucified again,
> Twice pierced his Gospel-bearing feet,
>   Twice broken his great heart, in vain.'
> I hear, and to myself I smile,
> For Christ talks with me, all the while."

XVIII

" THE GIFT OF A DAY "

THE burden of the day is often enough in our thoughts ; and the duty of the day is not likely to be forgotten ; but what we constantly overlook is the much happier, and equally true idea of the gift of a day. We receive a valuable present every morning—for the most part, thanklessly. We ask God to " give us this day our daily bread," and we return Him thanks for that when it is set before us. But which of us remembers that He gives, not only the bread, but the day as well ? Suppose we stand aloof from our day for a little, and try to realise what sheer bounties it brings us.

Stevenson declares that when a man who has got well into the seventies " lays his old bones in bed for the night, there is an overwhelming probability that he will never see the day." Even for the most youthful, however, sleep, when you think of it, is a hazardous adventure. " So far as our personality is concerned," says J. Brierley, in his " Our City of God," " we die every twenty-four hours." Yet the spirit returns

102

to its tabernacle, we awake again exactly to what
we left last night, with never a gape in the seam
to show the joining.   Who brings me, what brings
me back ?   Perfectly sure I am that I had nothing
to do with it.   I received a precious gift this
morning.   Some One has given me this day.

Moreover, it is not yesterday we get back, but
a new day.   You went to bed last night tired and
worn.   And when God brought you His gift this
morning, behold, He had smoothed out all the
weariness, and added strength and energy.   Not
in the last River of Death only is God with us,
but in this other black river that is so like it, the
river we cross to come to morning.   And this is
the token of His presence and His care of us
during the passage, that we drop so much of
yesterday's burden and weariness by the way.

When we think of what the day brings, too,
we are compelled to recognise the pure unmerited
grace of the giving.   When our eyes open on a
spring morning, how boundless are the riches
within reach of the poorest of us !   The air, the
sky, the sea, the song of the birds, and the scents
and colours of spring—all priceless things, and all
your very own if you have the heart to appreciate
them.   You may have them, says God, if you
can only see them.   There's nobody so poor that
he cannot afford a spring day.   Each morning

God puts a sheaf of blessed possibilities into our hands saying, " There, my child, these are for you, if you will." Each morning we rise to a clean sheet on which we may write what we please. We have the chance to learn, the chance to be kind, the chance to work, the chance to pray. This morning it was a blank cheque we got, valid for just as much as we liked to take.

We think with shame of the time we have lost and wasted, we grow sad as we look back at the chances we have missed, when, lo ! the message of the new day comes with its hope and its cheering. " Here," it says to you and me, " here is another chance ! It's not too late yet ! Opportunity, having shown you the warning written on her back, has returned. Yesterday you were sad and gloomy. To-day is your chance to prove yourself an unconquerable soul. Yesterday, you spoke unkindly to your friend. To-day, you can go and tell him you are sorry. Yesterday, you were churlish. To-day, if you will, you can be kind." Every morning, God in His mercy lets us begin again. " Are there not twelve hours in the day ? "—an ample allowance. Remember that, when you are feeling old and fear that your chance is past ; and let Hope come to you, as it ought to do, with God's new bounty of a day. To all men, Opportunity returns every morning.

Perhaps there is a hidden blessing in the fact that God's gift is only a day, that we are tenants of life only for the time between sleep and sleep. Round His gift, God has built the fence of night and unconsciousness, as if each day were meant, as we know indeed it is meant, to stand by itself and carry only its own burden and responsibility. This, then, is a true wisdom :—

> Build a little fence of trust
>   Just around to-day ;
> Fill the space with loving work,
>   And therein stay.
> Look not through the sheltering bars
>   Upon to-morrow.
> God will help thee bear whatever comes
>   Of joy or sorrow.

The gift of a day being what it is, surely we cannot maintain an indifferent attitude towards the Giver of it ? What we receive each morning, indeed, is a sacred and solemn trust. How base it were, then, to abuse it, to spend any part of our day in ways from which He who gives it must avert His Face !

Let us gather our thoughts together now, and not dismiss these lessons from our minds till we have joined in this prayer :—

" Our Father in Heaven, who bringest us back in safety from the far journey of sleep, and givest us the day, we thank Thee for all the bounties in Thy gift, and we ask Thy help that we may spend our day in Thy way and fear. When we grow despondent and weary, and reckon our chances gone, give us the grace to hear Thy Word of Hope that comes with each new day. When, through the bars of to-day, we seek to forecast the burdens of to-morrow, let Thy gracious promise that as our day is, so shall our strength be, keep our hearts in peace. And even as we lay us down to sleep this night in trust that Thou wilt keep us through the hours of darkness, and bring us, if it be Thy Will, to morning; so may we lie down at the last night of all, hoping on a new morn to awake again, and to be still with Thee, according to Thy word and witness to us in Christ Jesus, our Lord. Amen."

" Bear ye one another's burdens, and so fulfil the law of Christ."

(GALATIANS vi. 2.)

" Every man shall bear his own burden."

(GALATIANS vi. 5.)

" Cast thy burden upon the Lord."

(PSALM lv. 22.)

XIX

BURDENS

MOST of us know by experience what it means to bear a burden, and we naturally expect that the Bible should have something to say about it.   It has.   In two verses in Galatians and one in the Psalms, you have the whole philosophy and practice of burden-bearing set forth.

The first precept in this Christian art is " Bear ye one another's burdens, and so fulfil the law of Christ."   What a royal word that is !   *Fulfil* the law of Christ !   Surely that is something beyond the power of any one of us to do ?   How may I fulfil the law of Christ ?   By lending your brethren a hand with their burdens.   It seems marvellously simple, and yet, when you get it done to you, how great a thing it appears !   You never forget the hand that was reached out to you in your hour of darkness or despair.   And when you hear it said that being kind in that fashion is, for Christ, half the sum of all religion, you at least, I take it, do not feel inclined to dispute the statement. Religion for you then, in this aspect of it, just means passing on the gift you have received, speaking a cheerful word to the depressed, helping the troubled, sympathising with those who are sad.

> The world is wide, these things are small,
> They may be nothing, but they are all.

Opportunities for the exercise of this aspect of religion are never far away from any one of us. We find them lying where the Samaritan, in Christ's story, found his—at our feet. The whirligig of circumstance brings them to us or us to them. "A certain Samaritan, as he journeyed," said Christ. On other roads that day there were perhaps wayfarers in need of help, but the Samaritan fulfilled the law of Christ simply by attending to the one he came across. No one heart can gather into itself all the sorrow or pain in the world. It takes God's heart for that. But, as we journey, we come upon a brother to whom a helping hand would mean salvation, or a kindly, cheery word would be a means of grace. The law of Christ invites us to give that hand and speak that word. When we happen across some poor soul sitting, by reason of his infirmities, in gloom and darkness, and by any word or act of ours we can let God's sunlight into his soul, the will of Christ for you and me is that we try to do it. That is social service. That is real neighbourliness. And it is more. It is the fine fruit and most lovely flower of pure and undefiled religion.

The second article in the practice of burden-bearing is " Every man shall bear his own burden." There is no more precious gift than sympathy, but, curiously enough, the Word of God says more about giving sympathy than asking it for oneself. The practice of all the experts in the great art of living has been along this line, to hide their hurt or sorrow from the eyes of men rather than, by exhibiting it, to secure their sympathy. One has only to compare a brave reticence of this sort with what one sees sometimes of its opposite—a voluble sorrow, a patient who takes his troubles to every listener, a burdened soul whose woes are proclaimed upon the house-tops—to learn which is the truer ideal. A grief that is much handed about among friends is apt to become tawdry and soiled ; and in this connection one can see the meaning and approve the nobility of Bagshot's maxim, " Never show your wound except to a physician."

One must be careful, of course, not to overstate the matter here, and set up an ideal of self-sufficiency and reserve which is unnatural and wrong. But there are at least two good reasons why practice should lean to this side rather than the other. In the first place, because outward expression often reacts upon feeling and makes the trouble worse. Many a minor sorrow, at least, if kept secret would disappear of itself. Once expressed, however, it takes on an objective existence, and lives in spite of you. But a far better reason is the second, namely, that the world in which you live has sorrows enough of its own already. It is a sufficient condemnation of the practice of speaking of your ailments and symptoms to any who will listen that in many cases it is simply unkind, since they may be silently suffering something very much worse. Unless it is necessary to speak of it, why should you add to the world's gloom? And if it is, often times, wrong to speak of your bodily ailments, it is just as bad to speak of your doubts. Show your faith to the world and your friends, for they need all the inspiration you can give them, but keep your doubts to yourself, or reveal them only to your spiritual adviser.

Now, admittedly, this would be very austere and stoical doctrine if the Bible had no more to tell us of burden-bearing than that. But it

has more. The third and last article in the
Bible's philosophy and practice of burden-bearing is, " Cast thy burden upon the Lord." That
is a door which is always open. You cannot
go there too often, or with too ordinary and
common a sorrow. The trouble that is laid before God, though it be every day for long years,
never grows tawdry or soiled. Rather, like a
field spread out daily under His gracious sun, it
ripens and yields, in life and character, something of peaceable fruit. The disablements and
fears which, for their sakes, you hide from
your fellows, you may take there with a
perfect confidence. The world may misunderstand you and under-rate your burdens. But
you will never be rebuffed or heard impatiently
there.

We know that God is great, infinite, incom-
prehensible. We need nobody to teach us that.
But Jesus stands for the fact that God is little
too. When we read how God stooped to enter
man's estate in Bethlehem long ago, and laid
His hands on little children, and turned the
sorrow of this and that humble home into gladness, and dealt gently with a timid disciple who
stole to His side with questions one summer's
night, when you think of that, you need not
fear that the burdens you take to Him are

too small for His notice, or that He disdains to help you to bear them bravely. The fact of Christ is the eternal witness that Almighty God has stooped, and will stoop to your little burden and mine.

" *Whatsoever things are true,*
. honest, . . . just, . .
pure, . . . lovely, . . . of
good report ; if there be any
virtue, and if there be any
praise, think on these things."
(PHILIPPIANS iv. 8.)

XX

THE FURNISHING OF THE INNER CHAMBER

IT is a common criticism of the Christian religion that it makes for a narrow and restricted life, full of prohibitions and Thou shalt not's, and cutting a man off from much that is interesting and pleasant and profitable. Of course, it is a mistaken idea, though it has to be confessed that some Christian people lend it an appearance of truth by their manner of living and the ideals which they pursue. Nevertheless, the criticism is a libel. There is no man who has a nobler or wider heritage of liberty than the Christian. He has been made a freeman of a kingdom whose lines go out to the ends of the earth. In support of that contention I ask you to look at the catalogue which the Apostle Paul writes out, of the mental furnishing of the Christian man. I will tell you, he says, the furniture that ought to be found in the inner chamber of a Christian man's mind. Then follows the list :—"Whatsoever

H   113

things are true, whatsoever things are honest,
whatsoever things are just, whatsoever things
are pure, whatsoever things are lovely, whatsoever things are of good report, if there be any
virtue, and if there be any praise, think on these
things."

Will anybody say that that is a restricted
and provincial programme of interests ? Is there
any good thing in this life that is not included ?
As I read it, there is only one interest that is not
there, and that is sin, whatsoever worketh evil,
harms soul or body, or causeth a brother to offend.

But you will misunderstand the Apostle's
idea if you take him to mean that these are the
things that a Christian is permitted to think
about. He does not say that. He says these are
the things which he must think about. It is a
command, not a permission. Think only about
what is true and pure and just and lovely. Why ?
Isn't the Apostle taking a somewhat extreme view
in being so particular to make sure that our
thoughts are high and worthy ? If our actions
are right, and our speech is fitting, is that not
all that can be expected ? No, that is not enough,
for this reason—that it is our thoughts that most
of all determine what we are. Just as water
cannot rise above its own level, so we cannot rise
above the level of our secret habitual thoughts.

There is a verse in Proverbs which puts nearly the whole of modern psychology in a nutshell, " As a man thinketh in his heart, so is he." It is a moral impossibility for one who in his secret heart loves and welcomes all high and gracious and noble things, to be living a low and sordid and dishonourable life. His surroundings may be mean and unlovely, but it is the secret thoughts that make the man, far more than the environment. It is equally impossible for one whose mind is like a nest of unclean birds to be living a high and pure moral life. The thing is not merely beyond his wishes, it is beyond his power.

We may not be very sure where what is called original sin came from at the first, but there is not one of us who does not know how evil appears in our own life. It begins in thought about it. We turn the wrong thing over in our mind, we think of ourselves as doing it, long before it emerges as an actual deed or speech. Thomas A Kempis in his " Imitatio Christi" declares that the genesis of temptation is that " first there cometh to our minds the bare thought of evil." When that stage arrives, the battle has already begun. We strengthen our character, or we weaken it, by the things we think about.

For, and this is the important matter, our habitual thoughts work themselves out in our life. You remember how Ezekiel, in a vision, surprised the ancients of Israel at their unworthy worship in a dark underground chamber, offering incense to the pictures upon its walls. That sort of worship can only be kept secret for a while. Sooner or later it appears in a man's life what the things are which he cherishes and worships in his inner chamber. Our thoughts write themselves on our life, as the tippler's habits declare themselves in his bleary eyes and trembling hands, or as the saint's prayers purify and refine her face. There is no wiser petition in the Bible than the Psalmist's "Cleanse thou me from secret faults." For all the faults that bring men to shame were secret faults once upon a time. They begin in the dark, hidden and secret, but, like the plant's roots, they do not abide thus. By and by they send up shoots into the light where all men can see. The man who waves his censer to Mammon in his private chamber is known as a worldling, as the years go on, by other and more visible tokens. The impure mind teaches the tongue to speak its ideas, if you give it time enough. Jealousy, spite, and uncharitableness boil over some day. For there is nothing covered that shall not be revealed, neither hid that shall not be known.

For, mark you—and it is necessary to remember

this—God has given us freedom in this respect. I can't choose my surroundings, but I can choose my thoughts. I can't hinder evil entering my mind, but I need not, unless I like, bid it welcome and ask it to stay. I can get rid of it best, not by direct attack, but by what soldiers call a flank movement. To face the evil thoughts in your own mind, and try to think them away, is, in most cases, to make the trouble worse by concentrating attention upon it. The better way is Paul's—whatsoever things are true, pure, lovely, and of good report, think on these things. The good will expel the evil. An artist who visited a young undergraduate in his rooms was rather shocked to see the type of print and photograph with which his chamber was adorned. But he said not a word to him. Instead, he sent him a present, one of his own paintings, a beautiful symbolic piece of Christian art, with the request that he would hang it up in his room. As he despatched the gift, the artist remarked to himself, " That should banish the ballet-girls." And it did.

There is a wonderful fact about each of us which is as real as our shadow and as little thought about, namely, our unconscious influence upon others. Beyond all that we say or do, the self within us somehow speaks to all those whom we

meet.   There is a sort of magnetism, of one kind
or other, either attractive or repelling, about
us all.   It is a very strange thing, but it is a fact.
I do not suppose there is one of us who, if he might
choose, would not wish this kind of influence of
his upon others to be of a good and helpful sort.
But we can't make our unconscious influence to
order.   That is the difficulty.   It is quite beyond
our control, because, you see, it is quite unconscious.   But the thing that makes it what it is,
whether good or evil, we CAN deal with.   Do you
know what that is ?   Just our secret, cherished
thoughts.   Beyond our speech, they speak for
us.   Beyond our profession, they declare what
we are.   Wherefore, if, beyond all we do, we wish
to influence others for the things that are good
and true and pure, in our inmost hearts we must
love these things, choose and cherish them as the
furniture of our inner chamber.   If, beyond our
poor speech and imperfect discipleship, we want
our lives to speak for Christ, we must love Him
and worship Him, and cleave to Him, first in
our inmost hearts.   For, whatever we may profess, no man's life can speak for Christ, in whose
INNER sanctuary the place where Christ's image
should be, is empty.

XXI

THE OTHER LITTLE SHIPS

MOST of us, when we read the story of the Stilling of the Tempest on the Lake, overlook the fact that there were along with the disciples' boat "other little ships." Mark, however, specially notes this circumstance, and it suggests ideas worth considering. For, there must have been a storm for them also. Possibly the other boats belonged to fishermen plying their calling, or to friends and followers of Christ. Anyhow, they encountered the storm ; and they shared too in the peace which followed the sudden squall.

I think that suggests this thought—that God's blessings have a way of overflowing. It is not enough that He should deliver the boat which contains the disciples. At the same time, with the surplus of His bounty, He will save the other little ships as well. Even in material things, as you know, it is difficult to draw the line and say, Here the blessing ends. When an Admiralty order comes to the Clyde, it is not only the firm that builds the ship which reaps the benefit.

Many small tradesmen and humble housekeepers know better times, who have nothing whatever to do with ship-building. But in higher levels the feature becomes much more visible. Think of the preachers, the poets, the prophets of the Unseen who have most blessed and helped you. It was God who gave them these gifts ; but you and many others have been enriched because God was good to them. That indeed is the only real sort of Election. There is no question that " God elects some." But never merely for themselves. Always with His eye on others to be blessed through them. My idea of election is that when God delivered the disciples' boat from its distresses, He was thinking also of the other little ships alongside who were to share in the deliverance. We say that God elected Israel, as indeed He did. But not for Israel's own sake merely. Even we in this year of grace are like little ships in the neighbourhood of that ark, for we are still seeing God in these Hebrew scriptures, and praising Him in Israel's psalms. His Blessing has overflowed.

That is why it never perplexes me to find, outside of the Church and the profession of religion altogether, occasional beautiful characters and noble lives. It is in line with God's law in other spheres that the world should be enriched and sanctified with the overflow of His favour to those who are called by His Name. That is merely another instance of Grace which has broken bounds. These are some of the other little ships, sharing, though they know it not, in the disciples' blessing. These are wind-blown seeds from the Garden of the Lord.

Now change the point of view a little. When those in the disciples' boat awoke to a sense of their danger, and, through the presence of Christ, saved themselves from shipwreck, they had done more than they knew. They had saved the other little ships also. They were, indeed, responsible for those others as well as for themselves.

Now that is a fact which runs through the whole of life. A man who was hill-climbing with his boy, was once made to think very hard, and resolve on certain changes in his habits, by a remark which his son flung forward to him as they scaled a steep place in single file. "Take care, father," he said, "for I am following in your steps." There are rocks you know of, fathers, that you can maybe steer near to, without hurt. But there are other little ships coming along in your wake. What about them? Can they do it? And if they don't, whose is the responsibility?

Every man, however obscure, has his following; but it is specially worth the Christian man's while to remember that there are with him other little ships. "For their sakes," said Jesus once, "I sanctify myself." Whether we realise it or not, there is always this vicarious element in all Christian living. Growl and grumble, and you make life harder for others about you. Face it with a quiet trust in God, in the faith and fellowship of Jesus, and you call out a similar faith on all sides of you. However poor you esteem your influence, it is a fact that there are those who are taking their notions of Christian living from you, whose ideals will tumble as you lower yours. What, after all, is the Christian life but "having Christ on board your boat?" And when that is so, then, both in Galilee and in your own town, both in storm and in calm, something comes, something of blessing and helpfulness ought to come, to the little ships alongside. For that is a responsibility of which no disciple of Jesus Christ can ever possibly divest himself.

Change the point of view again. It was in answer to the prayer of the disciples that deliverance came also to those in the other little ships. They were saved by faith, but not by their own faith. They were blessed in answer to prayer, but it was not their own prayer. We have in this an almost perfect figure in the value of intercessory prayer.

And in the New Testament you find other instances of this same truth. Do you remember how Christ once blessed a Syrophœnician daughter because her mother's faith was strong? Do you remember how Christ once healed a paralytic when he saw the faith of the four men who carried his bed? The blessing of the other little ships is exactly in line with these.

This is a kind of prayer—it is the highest kind, indeed—about which the natural man is rather incredulous, and even devout people are sometimes not very sure. But the curious thing is that in these days of ours, confirmation and support for it are coming from quite an unexpected quarter. For psychic investigation, which seems to be giving us glimpses into other mysteries, is at present teaching us the reasonableness and the value of this very form of prayer. We are being told to-day by the youngest of the Sciences that you really do a great deal for a man when you send out to him, like wireless messages, your hopes and desires and prayers to God for his welfare. We now know at least quite certainly that we cannot measure, and we must not talk as if we could measure, the spirit forces that stream out in beneficent radiations from the heart of a praying man or woman.

And from all this, Christian people can at any-rate take fresh courage to believe that they can really further the causes and help the friends they love by their prayers for them. That never was doubted, of course, by those who were in the secret of the Lord. But it looks as if our newest science were going to shame the unbelief of many who profess themselves of the school of Christ. Our usefulness is greater than we realise. We are our brother's keeper in a wider sense than we think. If his heart is hard and his eyes holden. we ask, and we have pleaded with him in vain, is not our responsibility at an end ? Must it not be unto him according to his faith or want of faith at the last ? No, we have touched a deeper truth than that to-day—and don't let us forget it ; it may be unto my brother yet according to MY prayer and MY faith.

*" Take therefore no thought
for the morrow."*

(MATTHEW vi. 34.)

XXII

WORRY

THE power of religion to deal with such a common and clamant evil as worry must constitute a crucial test of its worth. I wish to say at once that I believe it can stand the test. A famous psychologist has said, " The sovereign cure for worry is religious faith." I am writing in the conviction that that is true. The question of the surgeon in Tennyson's poem, " The Children's Hospital "—" Can faith set a broken bone ? " we can only answer frankly in the negative. Broken bones lie outside of Faith's beneficent influence altogether. But to the question—Can faith rid the mind of worry ? the only answer which is true to fact is Yes, it can ! It is almost the only cure there is.

Nearly every one knows how multifarious are the interests round which worry, like an evil growth, can gather itself. " I write," says the medical author of a monograph on this subject, " for those who fear forty and grey hairs, and consumption and cancer and death, and beyond

all that, the chance of something after death."
If only he gets his due, what a multitude of eager
readers this writer should have ! There are many
people who never relax their inward grip of themselves from morning to night. When one worry
has proved groundless—which is a common
enough occurrence, since a large proportion of
the troubles we foresee never as a matter of fact
happen—or when it is forgotten, another takes
its place before the convulsive strained self has
time to rest.

Most of us know well enough what the con-
sequences are—inefficiency, a paralysis of one's
best efforts, a discount from health if one be otherwise well, and an increase of the trouble, if one
be ill. Worry, in fact, does what work alone
cannot do, it can kill, and does kill its thousands
every year.

Worry in many of its forms is so closely con-
nected with a strongly-developed consciousness
of Self as to be practically indistinguishable
from it. One's worries can often be explained
by the fact that Self is bulking too largely in
one's thoughts. No cure can be effective, therefore, which does not deal radically with this too
forward self, put it in its place, and keep it there.

Practical psychologists can help us a little to
get rid of the tension of nerve and mind which

is one of worry's symptoms. We are told to
relax our muscles, to breathe deep and slowly,
to express courage and equanimity outwardly,
and our inward mood will come to correspond—
all very wise, no doubt, and interesting for those
who like to try new tricks upon themselves.
But we are saved the necessity of pointing out
that these things, at best, are but painting the
pump to improve the quality of the water, by
the confession of one of the greatest of that
school of teachers, the late Prof. William James,
whose words we have already quoted, that " the
sovereign cure for worry is religious faith."

What, then, is the worried man to have for
a faith ? I reply, the fact that God is our watchful, all-wise and loving Father. The man who
can let himself go so far as to lean all his weight
on that, in simple trust, is on the road to the
cure of worry.

It is not a difficult thing to believe. Thousands of people have given their assent to it. It
was the faith of our Lord Jesus Christ, and it
is His Gospel of good news to us. Your
Father knoweth. Your Father loveth. Your
Father cares.

If you can accept a truth because it comes
from Christ, take that into your life. Believe
that God cares for you and wills for you only

the best. When you have done all in your power
to succeed in your calling and to fill your niche
in life, leave the result confidently with God.
When you have taken all due and proper care of
it, your health is as He ordains. If you are to
die, die like a brave man, with your face to God
and your hope in His Mercy. You can do no
more, and "underneath are the everlasting
arms." But do not, in craven fear of death, die
every day. If people slight you and requite you
ill, misunderstand you and pass you by, call to
your aid the thought of God lavishing His care
even on the tiniest insect He has made. He will
not overlook you, or pass you by. Just a little
way up on the heights of faith in God, what your
friend said of you, how your rival misrepresents
you, how your neighbour treats you, will seem
very small affairs. Cast your burden, whatever
it be, upon the Lord, and go and do the thing
that you know to be right.

Then, indeed, you can "unclamp." Then you
can relax, and have some ground for it—relax
your anxious, convulsive grip of self, and all
the agony and strain of playing Providence to
yourself. No need any more to sleep with one
eye open, on the watch for the blow that is ever
about to fall, and the disaster that is hanging by
a hair. God is your Providence now, and not

yourself. You have left all care and chance with Him. And by all the experience of thousands of your fellows, your faith will be justified by its results. You will be free. Even when the blow has fallen and the surface of life is storm-tossed and broken—for there is no promise that trouble will not come your way, as it does to others—you will find within yourself, in some degree, like the placid deeps in a wind-vexed sea, a Christ-like peace of heart.

You have heard the phrase, " dying with Christ." Did you ever think out what meaning that can have for you ? It means forgetting yourself, it means letting your purely self-regarding life die. And how may one learn it ? Not in a day, nor perfectly even in a lifetime. But of all Christ's true and earnest disciples it can be said that they are learning it. Just as the boy grows like the hero he elects, just as between husband and wife there sometimes develops a strange likeness even to feature, so those into whose mind and heart the thought of Christ often comes as an inspiration and a standard of living, grow like Him even to the forgetting of self. They are constrained to strive to displace self and enshrine in its room the ideal of Jesus. They try to think of others in their joys and sorrows. They try to serve Christ in the service of others,

I

where and when and how they can. They learn to pray to be made of use, and they keep their eyes open for chances. The remedy for undue self-regard is a vision of how much nobler, truer, and more useful the self-forgetful life is. That vision is always open to us all in the Gospel of Jesus Christ.

To leave our cares with God our Father who loves us, and to learn from Jesus to forget ourselves, will cure worry. The motto of the method is given memorably in these words, which may be commended as a daily text for all who are addicted to worrying : " Look up, not down; look forward, not back ; look out, not in ; and lend a hand."

*" Wisdom is before him that
hath understanding ; but the
eyes of a fool are in the ends of
the earth."*

(PROVERBS xvii. 24.)

XXIII

THE EYES OF A FOOL

" WISDOM," says the author of Proverbs, " is
before him that hath understanding, but the
eyes of a fool are in the ends of the earth." By
wisdom the Hebrew meant all that goes to make
life stable, joyous, and blessed ; and that, says
Solomon, does not need to be sought for in remote
and inaccessible places. It lies right in a man's
path. It is to be picked up at his feet. But the
foolish man overlooks it there so obviously ; his
eyes are in the ends of the earth.

I take this to mean, for us, that there are great
gifts in life, things good and useful which we
shall altogether miss if we look for them where
the fool looks. We need them so much that
God has set them near us all.

One of these gifts is DUTY, one of life's quiet
blessings, and its greatest steadying influence.
God has placed that day by day into the hands
of each of us. With the gift of work to do,
we have got also a law as to how it is to be
done, a law written in conscience and revela-

tion alike, namely, that the nearest is to be done first.

Yet Duty is just one of the things which we are all tempted to look for in the ends of the earth. If the nearest duty does not happen to be the most agreeable, there are very few of us who are not tempted to scan the horizon round in order to find a more pleasant, though remote, one which might take its place. How easy other people's duty seems at times compared with ours! How much more interesting their daily task is than the treadmill round in which we spend our days! Recognise that fact, if you must; admit the truth of it, if you will, when the mood is on you; but beware of yielding to it and putting aside the thing that lies to your hand, for out of that yielding is born the busybody, the prig, and, in the end, the coward. Duty, however prosaic a face it bear, is a royal word among the words of earth, stamped in the mint of heaven, and supreme above all feelings or moods or inclination. That disciple has learned much who recognises in the nearest duty, drab and dusty though it be, God's call to him to play the man, God's approach to him with purpose of blessing, nay more, that very manifestation of His Spirit for which we all pray. For there is no one with any sense of God but asks, " Show me Thy ways,

O Lord ? " But how many realise that in the plain duty lying right in our path, God is sending, day by day, His answer ?

When we read the story of our Lord's life from this point of view, how deft and unhurried appears His handling of it ! No tension and no postponement, but each day's opportunity and ministry quietly accepted and fulfilled. Something like the explanation of it is seen when we notice how the word " first " on Christ's lips rings through the whole of the Gospels—" first take the beam out of thine own eye," " first be reconciled to thy brother," " first gird thyself and serve," " first the Kingdom of God and His righteousness." Christ was supremely loyal to the order of duty, and in His " firsts " we can see our highests and our nearests, to be striven after, not in some other far-off ideal condition, but in these very ordinary surroundings of ours and in that daily life " which is the life of all of us."

There is another gracious gift of God that we are all prone to seek far out from where we dwell, namely, HAPPINESS. Mark you, I do not speak of Joy. Joy is the atmosphere that surrounds life's great and sacramental moments. It is the air about the mount of God. But happiness is a more familiar and intimate thing. It can enfold the very humblest home. It may wrap a man round like a benediction what time he sings at his task. It may be struck out on a sudden, like fire from a flint, at the smile of a friend. Often enough we recognise it only when its back is turned, and then analysis is difficult, but again and again I am sure we have marvelled to see how small a thing it takes to make us happy, how familiar and intimate are the conditions within which it condescends to dwell.

Yet how many are looking for it in vain in the ends of the earth! To travel in search of heart's-ease and the quiet blessing of happiness is surely foolish, since it is to be had much nearer at hand. To think to achieve it by exchange of lots with some one whose circumstances seem more promising is the vainest of dreams. You may believe, like the child in the story, that the house with the golden windows lies on the other side of the valley from your own, but if you were to go there you would find, as he did, that it is your own home whose casements are ablaze with the light of the westering sun. Yours, my brother, is the home that has the golden windows. Happiness for you, if anywhere, lies just there, in your home's welcome and trust and gaiety, in the sound of the voices that you love, in your daily work and nightly rest. If you cannot find it there,

you will never discover it anywhere else. As
Stevenson reminds the grumbler—

> " The shoon ye coft, the life ye lead,
>   Ithers will heir when aince ye're deid;
> They'll heir your tastless bit o' breid,
>   An' find it sappy;
> They'll to your dulefu' house succeed,
>   An' there be happy."

Perhaps it was a grotesque thing for Smetham
to refuse to go with some friends to Rome because
he had not yet exhausted the beauties of his own
garden, but it seems to me that the secret of
happiness, as it is ministered to by the world of
God around us, lies nearer to Smetham than to his
friends. Happiness, also, is before him that hath
understanding, but the eyes of a fool are in the
ends of the earth.

And best of all, we need not seek in far-away
places to find God. Jesus has opened our eyes
to the truth that God is a Spirit, not confined in
any temple made with hands, but to be worshipped
and communed with anywhere and everywhere,
by all who desire and need His Presence.

As if to bring that truth home to all whom His
Gospel might reach, the story of that perfect life
is full from end to end of tokens that, for Jesus,
God the Father was ever just beside Him, for He
found Him, and showed Him to men, in the

flowers of the field, in the wind among the tree-tops overhead, in the seed and the harvest, and in all the varied business and duty of ordinary life. Each parable of Jesus has its own lesson, but the lesson of them all taken together is that God is not afar off, but rather that

> " Earth's crammed with Heaven,
> And every common bush afire with God."

Men turn to the east at the mention of Christ's name, as if He belonged there in special fashion still. They forget that He said, " It is expedient for you that I go away." And why expedient ? Because if He were in Palestine still, as Henry Drummond once said, only a few could hope for His fellowship. But the world of spirit into which He has gone is as universal and all-permeating as the air we breathe. Wherever man is, it is about him. And so our Master's new word is, " Lo, I am with you alway, even unto the end of the world."

" Closer is He than breathing, and nearer than hands and feet."

" In the noise and clatter of my kitchen," said Brother Lawrence, " where several persons are together calling for as many different things, I possess Him in as great tranquillity as when upon my knees at the blessed Sacrament."

Prof. A. B. Davidson has a very suggestive remark about the Person like unto the Son of God who was seen with the three in the fiery furnace. He notes that it is not said that THEY saw Him. Though Christ says He is always with those who love Him and try to serve Him, He does not say that they will always feel or always realise His presence. Yet, realised or not, His promise stands, that He is nearer than Jerusalem, nearer than the church in which we worship Him, even in spirit touching our spirits at all times, so that whoso is tempted may have Him for helper, and whoso is lonely may have Him for friend.

Duty and happiness we need for normal living, so God has set them, not at the ends of the earth, but very near to us all. But since there is another need of sinful men greater than either, " If any man open the door," says Christ the Saviour " I will come in." God is as near as that.

" His windows being open in his chamber toward Jerusalem."
(DANIEL vi. 10.)

XXIV

THE OPEN WINDOW

WHEN Daniel, in spite of the grim decree of Darius, made his prayer to his God beside the window that opened towards Jerusalem, his choice was determined not only by the fact that Jerusalem was his own early home, but far more by the fact that it was pre-eminently the city of God, the place where His Temple was, and where Daniel believed that He came nearest to His people. When Daniel opened the window that looked towards Jerusalem he was opening it towards all that he knew and believed about God. He deliberately chose for his favourite view the window whose outlook was towards the highest that life held for him.

That choice is also in our power. The chamber of our soul has its windows also, facing this way and that. We are each of us free to choose which we shall open and keep open. We can shut out a view that displeases us. We can select what we prefer. Most of us have to be content with the view which we get from the windows of our homes, and, if that be not to our liking, it may not be quite so easy as it sounds to change it. But not one of God's children need look from his soul's windows upon pigstyes or rubbish heaps unless he wants to. They are there of course, if he prefers them. There are material and sordid views of life and character that will enfeeble faith and rob holy things of their sacredness and drag his ideals in the mire. They are to be found in books and to be learned from men and women ; and if you open your window on these things they will do their evil work upon you, filling the whole chamber of your soul with their suspicion and their bleak despair. But you don't need to choose that window. There are others that are equally free and infinitely more inspiring. There are books that strengthen all that is worthy and pure and true. There are friends whose fellowship is a benediction. You can open your window to these. You can cultivate these. You can seek them deliberately. Even though Babylon's voice be loud, and Jerusalem seem a great way off, it is better, yea, even if there be no Christ and no heaven it must still be better to choose for our soul's outlook the very highest that we know. For we have the choice. That liberty God gave us with the gift of life.

You are always free to open your window

towards Jerusalem, and Jerusalem is the City
of Christ. It was there He taught and showed
men the Father. It was there the Cross stood
that brings us, unworthy as we are, near to the
very Heart of God and Him to us. God you
cannot see, but Christ and His Cross you can.
That outlook is yours, if you choose. You can
say, " This is God for me, Jesus, who lived and
died for men." If you know of any more satisfy-
ing revelation of the heart and love of the Eternal,
choose it by all means. But if not, open your
window towards Jerusalem, and you will only be
doing what saint and sinner in all the ages past
have done. This, O my soul, is God for thee—
Jesus, " the shadow of Him, Love, the speech of
Him, soft music and His step a benediction."
Here is the God thou seekest come nigh, humbling
Himself to find thee, living to show thee how to
live, and dying to draw thee away from thyself
to God and Love and Him. Let me choose that,
of all windows, this one be opened for me, that I
may look and learn, that here too I may come
and pray, this window that looks towards the
unseen and eternal God, over the City of the Cross
of Christ.

I think Daniel's window often stood open. I
don't think he shut it when his hour of prayer
was past. As he sat in his chamber and worked

or read or simply dreamed, the spirit of his early home and his faith drew near and touched and helped him, though it were unconsciously, many times a day. The choice, in short, became a habit, and the habit brought him constant inspiration and strength and peace.

I want to say that that is the immediate and present blessing attached to the choice of the best window. Choose the best deliberately though it be with an effort; look for the good and beautiful and Godlike in life and your friends and your daily surroundings, and, by and by, you will find that the good and beautiful and Godlike are seeking you. The airs of heaven will often come and touch your cheek because your windows are open. Things that are lovely and of good report will announce themselves to you even where you do not expect them. Only lift up an unbarred heart towards the Highest that you know, as the flower holds up its petals to the sky, and all the day long God will touch it and tend it, now with a shaft of sunlight, now with the dew from heaven.

It is this habit of the open window that distinguishes those who possess the enviable power of seeing a soul of goodness even in things evil. At first they had to look for the goodness. But now it comes and calls aloud to them. Marks of heaven start up and announce themselves in lives that touch theirs every day. The gracious words and loving deeds that are making their own homes beautiful, they at least do not fail to see. It is they who have the eyes for the quiet heroisms of life, for the pain that is hidden by brave smiles. It is they who see unselfishness causing a face to shine, where others see a neighbour and nothing more.

They have their blessing and reward even now. They see the best in life, and the best shows itself to them. They entertain many an angel unawares, because their door is always open out upon the angel path. They are not always happy, but they are always blessed, and they bless others. They are always hopeful, believing in the best and finding it in strange places. Like those who hunger and thirst after righteousness, they have their blessing even now.

And like them, also, they shall have their final reward. For as those who so hunger and thirst shall at last be filled, those also who reach out towards the Best shall find it more and more. Daniel's exile is long since ended, and he dwells now in the City of God towards which he looked from his chamber in Babylon. Keep your window open towards the Highest, and you will come to it at the last.

XXV

"WHAT HAST THOU IN THE HOUSE?"

THIS is the question which Elisha asked
the destitute and poverty-stricken widow who
applied to him for help. Her reply was that
she had nothing save a pot of oil. Nevertheless he ordered her to borrow all the empty
vessels she could, and fill them out of her little
pot; and the story goes on to tell that she
did so, and found that all that she had were
filled.

Not without its initial difficulties for the
modern mind, this Old Testament story opens
up most suggestively when we make trial of its
meaning by way of the prophet's question—
" What hast thou in the house?" It leads on
to a great principle of Nature and of Grace of
which no one ought to be ignorant. God can
and will do wonderful things with but a small
store to work upon, but man must make his
contribution to the result. God is always ready
to fill all our vessels full, but we must first give
Him our little pot of oil. That, it seems to me,

is the lesson of the story ; and even the modern
man needs to hear it.

In a single grain of corn, what uncountable
possibilities lie ! Out of that one grain may come,
in the course of years, enough to feed a whole
country. There is a miracle there waiting to be
worked. Waiting, on what ? On the farmer
giving up that grain, offering it to God, dropping
it in the ground. Without that, no miracle is
possible at all. When you ask Nature to give
you a harvest, she asks you, " What hast thou in
the house ? "

If it be some new habit which you wish to form,
you must GIVE first, before you GET. You begin
with what you can do yourself. You contribute,
with great sweat and endeavour perhaps, the first
and second and third acts in the series ; and before
long you find that the habit has developed legs
and is able to walk. The empty vessels are being
filled with what beneficent Nature has ADDED
to your meagre contribution.

No one should be ignorant of the blessed truth
that there are simply limitless possibilities latent
within himself. There is not one of us living
up to a tithe of our powers, whether mental
or spiritual. There are empty vessels standing
round each of us, and all that we need in order to
fill them, out of God's fullness, is sufficient faith

in our own little pot of oil. You can run this up as high as you can see, and it is still true. Do you want to be fit for bigger duties? The result is quite certain if you contribute your present small duty, done as well as you can. Our Lord's own condition for a man ruling over many things is that he be faithful in a few. Does someone complain that his faith is weak? Let him act up to the faith and light he has at present, and he will surely find his store increased. The annals of all Christ's causes are full of instances of how He has taken the poor self-offering of willing men and women and blessed and multiplied that, as once he blessed and multiplied the loaves, till what they gave fed many hungry souls besides their own. That is a law that always holds true. It is a principle of God's universe, physical, moral, and spiritual, that never fails to work. Man's share is to provide the oil : God's is to bless and multiply that.

The pilgrim in Bunyan's allegory was shown, in the House of the Interpreter, a fire which, in spite of the water thrown on it, continued to burn because there was one behind the wall who constantly replenished it. There is always God behind the wall to feed our fire, if we but light it. When we look at our one poor talent, and ask what possible good can be done with that, don't

K

let us forget the One behind the wall. Beyond all our poor efforts, God adds to what we offer; He " giveth to His beloved while they sleep."

There are few things in life better worth remembering than that if a man is doing his clear duty, speaking the difficult truth, or in any way and sphere standing out for the Will of God, he has the whole agency of heaven at his back. Just as the seed calls to its aid all the forces of Nature, so does a man's brave word or resolute endeavour link itself on to all the Might of God. That is why the truth, though it be feeble to-day, shall yet rule the world. That is why no helpful, kindly word or deed shall ultimately fail of a great return. That is why no really good cause in this world can be finally cheated of its success. It is not that our poor efforts can fill these empty vessels ; it is that our little pot of oil calls upon God for His increase, and never calls in vain. If this ancient story helps us to believe that, it has justified its place in our Bible.

If we have the courage to believe that this miracle is possible in our lives, it will certainly be repeated. It is being repeated, indeed, all round us, every day. As surely as God and the acorn, which a man drops in the ground, together bring about a great and sturdy oak, so surely shall He increase and multiply the offering that you make to Him.

There are many men who would serve God and their fellows much more hopefully if they could catch sight of this great truth. They hang back and become discouraged because their pot of oil is so small. To all of us whose trouble that is, this ancient story brings its rare and bracing counsel: Use what you have got, and you will find it plenty! Begin to pour out your oil, and God will see to it that your vessels are filled!

" *Behold a ladder set up on the earth, and the top of it reached to heaven : and behold the angels of God ascending and descending on it.*"

(GENESIS xxviii. 12.)

" *Behold the mountain was full of horses and chariots of fire round about Elisha.*"

(2 KINGS vi. 17.)

XXVI

OUR UNSEEN ENVIRONMENT

IN one of his finest essays, William James deals with what he calls a certain blindness in human beings, blindness, that is to say, to what in a neighbour's experience constitutes the true taste of it. It is very little of the glorious, boyish romance of carrying a dark lantern, about which Stevenson has written, that is visible from the outside to the grown-up and staid observer. The settler's keen pleasure in subduing the wilderness is not known at all to the traveller who whisks past it in a train.

But the Bible asserts from end to end of it that there is a respect of far greater importance in which we are nearly all blind,—namely, to the fact that there is really far more in life than we can see or handle or measure. There is a spiritual realm beyond and around the visible, and not a great many have eyes for that. The

Bible does not seek to prove that.   It simply states
that it is so.   It takes it magnificently for granted.
And now and then it lets us see what happens
when men make the discovery that they are living
in an unseen spiritual environment.   Jacob, for
example, at Bethel made that discovery, learned
in his dream that even from where he lay there
stretched a ladder up to heaven.   Elisha's servant
at Dothan, mortally afraid of the encompassing
hosts of Syria, became a new man when his eyes
were really opened and he saw round about him
armies that were mightier still, the chariotry of
Heaven.

Over against our buying and selling and
our immersion in the affairs of this world, this
witness stands declaring, " There is something
more."   Across the world's self-satisfaction, its
love of comfort and its scramble for wealth, it
writes with a calm assurance, " Man liveth not
by bread alone."   And the only person whom
Jesus ever called a fool was a man who thought
he could.

Speaking about Ruskin, A. C. Benson says that
he saw the light ON things so clearly that he did
not see the hidden light that falls THROUGH them.
But does not the light ON things blind, and, for
a while, content us all ?   Then why bother about
the unseen and spiritual at all, some one says ?

Because, my brother, we cannot help ourselves. As well tell the plant in a cellar not to bother for the light of the sun. We were made for it. That is the fact. The trouble began far back when God created man " in His own image." And in spite of ourselves, our instincts come out sometime or other and set us groping for God. Materialism would long ago have become the universal creed, as it is the most obvious one, but for the fact that it goes all to pieces at our Bethels and our Dothans.

Further, the Bible tells us what the unseen and spiritual world is for—not merely to be God's dwelling-place and Home, but set there for the nourishment of man's soul. As he has air for his lungs, man has a spiritual environment for his soul. Both are of God's provision, for his children's need.

To try to be a spiritual man while living entirely in a material environment is about as hopeless a thing as it would be to try to grow roses without light or keep fish alive on air.

But isn't that just what many of us are trying to do? We eat and drink and play and work and sleep, and marvel that our souls are not strong, that our faith is fitful and our vision dim. How can it be otherwise? You can't nourish a soul on material things. We can gulp down lungfuls of air and not sensibly exhaust our supply. We can bask all day in the sun and not impoverish our neighbour of its blessing. And God's provision for our spiritual needs is on the same abundant scale. Yet it is only at rare intervals, if at all, we remember that beyond the desk in the city and our swift temptation, or beyond the loneliness of our sorrow, there is all the fullness of God and the companionship of Jesus, for every child of His that covets it.

The Bible particularises. It speaks of our environment as personal. We hear of a cloud of witnesses. Jacob saw that there were angels near about him where he lay. I have heard a man say that he felt his mother nearer him since she died than in the years of her living presence. Are we, because we do not know, to forbid that belief ? Nay, rather, shall not he adhere all the more loyally to what is high and noble, and resist his evil with a stouter heart who believes that, in the cloud of witnesses that compass him around, there be some to whom he is still dear, though they have gone from his sight, some who do more than watch as mere impartial spectators ? The truth is we are like blind men in a city, with life and movement all about us but beyond our ken. Sometimes we are helped at a difficult crossing. Sometimes we find a gift dropped into

our can, and sometimes when we would have
stumbled there is a strong hand upon our arm.
Sometimes into our sinful hearts there comes
a pure white thought, like a feather from some
passing wing. And we have given our thanks
to God, when these things have happened, believing, for we are blind, and cannot see, that
there are ministering spirits all around us and
never very far away.

The Bible lets us see very clearly the effect
upon weak and timid men of realising the presence of their spiritual allies and helpers. Jacob,
made aware of God and His guardian angels,
rises up and goes off a new man. Elisha's servant
sees the sun glinting on the arms of the Syrians
in quietness and confidence of heart.

It would make the same difference to us all.
It has done so to all those who, with no vision
of angels or chariots, have trusted in the help
of the Unseen with a trust they have learned
from Christ. They are quite sure that greater
is He that is for them than all those that can be
against them. And they are not afraid of the
terror by night nor of the arrow that flieth by
day, of the pestilence that walketh in darkness,
nor of the demon that destroyeth in the noon
day. They say, " The Lord is my Light and my
salvation, whom shall I fear ? He shall preserve

my going out and my coming in from this time
forth and even for ever more."

Or, in modern plain speech, it comes to this :
—There is a strength available for the very
weakest of us, if we seek it from God. The
very least of us is precious in the Father's sight,
and about us in all our goings are the everlasting
arms.   Christ is God's pledge that He is not
far off in His remote heaven, but about us here
and now ; and in every effort for the right, in
every struggle to be true, in every sore endeavour
towards the highest, we have aback of us a power
that is sufficient, because it comes from God.

XXVII

THE DAY'S WORK

IN that fine Nature-poem, the 104th Psalm, the contrast that is drawn between the animals and man is that, with the rising of the sun, these creep back to their dens, while he goeth forth to his work and his labour till the evening. It is his work, his day's work that proclaims him a being apart from all the other creatures of the Almighty. His glory is that he goeth forth to his work. There is nothing of the " curse of labour " here ! Instead, there appears the very poetry of work, work made glorious, and claimed as man's badge of honour.

Let us think of our work as making us co-workers with God. It is a most mischievous limiting of God to think of Him as interested only in the work we call religious. God's energy is as wide and manifold as the world which He has made, and His interest cannot be expressed any less widely. It was a fine note for Dale of Birmingham to strike when he wrote on " Every Day Business a Divine Calling." Since it is

God who created the timber and the iron and the cotton and all the other raw materials of commerce and handicraft, the men who are manufacturing or distributing these products need no further reminder that they are helping God. It is His Will that the wheat the farmer grows should be made into flour by the miller, sold by the grocer, and turned into bread by the baker. The whole progress of the world would come to an end if the only work which those who believe in God could properly do for Him were what we call religious work. God has need of men of business, of science, of letters, of art. He must have tradesmen and artificers in wood and iron and stone. Eighteen hundred years ago, it has been pointed out, there was no such country as the Holland of to-day. God has made it possible, but man had to give it frame and form. The Dutch navvy building Holland's dykes to keep the sea back from the reclaimed land, had his niche in the Universe and was doing what God could not do without him, as truly as any member of the greatest and most useful profession in the world.

Take that thought out with you to your work to-morrow morning, whatever that work be. Link it on to God's great plan of the Universe. Because it is man's work you are doing, dare to think of yourself as one of God's helpers, a co-worker with Him.

Let us think of our day's work, also, as that which establishes and solidifies character. We get our visions and ideals elsewhere, but they are " burned in " in the day's work. It is there we bring all our religion and all our theories and principles to the proof. " The harper," says Aristotle, " is not made otherwise than by harping, nor the just man otherwise than by doing just deeds." Precisely. And our day's work is the exercise-ground not only for justice, but for truth and honour, fidelity, courage, and all that goes to make a man. " A workshop," as Henry Drummond once said, " is not a place for making engines so much as a place for making men." It does not matter what a man's business or profession be, so long as it is clean and honour-able ; beyond all its value to society or the general weal is its value to himself as a discipline and battle-ground. In the very humblest manual calling as in the most coveted office there are opportunities for loyalty, for perseverance, for integrity, for self-control. And if God's great end with men be to fashion character, the sphere of the day's work, far from being outside of His view, must be regarded by Him with special in-terest and expectancy. It does not much matter under what trade or calling his name appears in the Directory, it's the exercise of courage, patience and kindness that is the significant part of a man's business in the sight of God. It is, as one has put it finely, " because we have to go, morning after morning, through rain, through shine, through toothache, headache, heartache, to the appointed spot and do the appointed work ; because, and only because, we have to stick to that work through the eight or ten hours, long after rest would be sweet ; because the schoolboy's lesson must be learned at nine o'clock, and learned without a slip ; because the accounts on the ledger must be square to a penny ; because the goods must tally exactly with the invoice ; because good temper must be kept with children, friends, customers, neighbours, not seven, but seventy times seven times ; because the besetting sin must be watched to-day and to-morrow and the next day, in short, without much matter what our work be, it is because, and only because, of the rut, grind, humdrum drudgery of the work that we at last get those self-foundations laid— attention, promptness, accuracy, firmness, patience, self-denial, and all the rest." There is no other way to get these things. And they are all indispensable for character.

Further, I think no one will underrate the

sacredness of his daily labour who remembers that Jesus Christ Himself spent so much of His life in just this way. Till the beginning of His brief public ministry, His day's work was the only sphere in which Jesus could show forth the glory of God. The fact that He worked sanctifies all work and every place where honest, useful work is done. We have not even yet begun to realise what that fact means—that He whom we call Saviour and Son of God should have spent the largest part of His life in the most humble and ordinary and, in itself, uninspiring toil. Certainly, for every worker, whatever be his task, who has once caught sight of the Son of God in the Carpenter's Shop at Nazareth, no calling, however humble or ordinary, can ever seem inglorious again.

The day's work, friends, is NOT time lost for religion, any more than the years Jesus spent in the workshop at Nazareth were time lost in His service of God. It IS religion. It may not be Church work, but then we need to learn that religion is a far wider and far greater thing than Church work. From its very nature, worship, services, church-attendance can only receive a portion of our time and attention, though it is a portion of the utmost importance, which we omit to our own loss. But religion must take all our

time, or it is not religion at all. If only all the busy
men and women who worship God upon the
Sunday went out to their work the next day as
certain that they were serving Him really and
acceptably there also, what a revolution there
would be! And why should they not? You
may search the Gospels through, and you will not
find the vestige of a tendency to apologise for
those years of Christ's spent beside the bench in
Nazareth. In the workshop, as truly as when
He preached the Sermon on the Mount, He was
fulfilling the Will of God, and discharging His
Sonship. And that redeems the day's work for
all His disciples. Wherever your work takes
you, into office, workshop, or market place, remember that Jesus has been in such a place as
that and served God there. And never doubt
that His calling of you as His disciple is His command to you to follow Him in that also.

> " Very dear the Cross of Shame
>   Where He took the sinner's blame,
>   And the tomb wherein the Saviour lay
>   Until the third day came ;
>   Yet He bore the self-same load,
>   And He went the same high road,
>   When the Carpenter of Nazareth
>   Made common things for God."

" *And the man of God was
wroth with him, and said, Thou
shouldest have smitten five or
six times.*"

(2 KINGS xiii. 19.)

XXVIII

THE GRACE OF GRIT

I ONCE heard about a keen golfer who, to rid
himself of a bad fault, had the maxim " Slow
back " written on a slip of paper, and stuck on
his mirror where he could see it every morning
when he was shaving. But I can think of a
better maxim than that to keep constantly before
one, good not only for golf but for the more
serious business of life, and that is " Follow
through." As the success of a drive depends
largely upon carrying the swing hard and clean
out to a finish, so success in any line is almost
assured if you follow through.

Grit is not a very pretty word, to be sure.
But it denotes an excellent quality. It is that
percentage of iron in a man's temperament that
gives stability and permanence to his character,
the " steel rod in his backbone " that prevents
him bending to every prompting of impulse, or
gust of fickle opinion. If he has that grace, no
matter what his other failings may be, you may
trust a duty to him, confident that he will see it

through somehow, and that you won't need to go and pick it up where he has left it half-done. Grit is that hard enduring something that you get down to when the strain comes. It is easy enough to attend a committee meeting for a time or two, to read the first chapters of a hard book, or begin a new habit. The flabbiest of mortals can do as much as that. Even Pliable ran well for a time. But it is afterwards, when the freshness of the experience has worn off, when the pull begins, when loyalty and steadfastness are called for, that grit, or the want of it, begins to show.

Grit is not merely a physical quality, not a case of muscle or bodily stamina. It has to do with the fibre of one's mind far more than with one's chest measurement. Before a man is beaten at his task, whatever it be—however much it may depend upon strength or skill— he is beaten first in his own mind.

Now it would be a depressing thing to say all this, or read it, if grit were simply a natural gift. But it is not so ; it can be cultivated, and it ought to be cultivated. Wasn't it Wordsworth who refused to turn in his walk when it threatened rain, on the ground that it would do him more harm morally to break a purpose he had once formed, than any bodily harm a wetting

L

might do ? A somewhat dangerous application, perhaps, but a sound principle, all the same.

" Keep the faculty of effort alive in you by a little gratuitous exercise every day," says an expert in psychology, " that is, be systematically ascetic or heroic in little unnecessary points, do, every day or two, something, for no other reason than that you would rather not do it, so that when the hour of dire need draws nigh, it may not find you unnerved and untrained to stand the test." Let no man despise these unimportant efforts at self-discipline. They make character, and character is not an unimportant thing. The man who by practice gets into the habit of standing by his guns till the engagement is over, has enormously increased his value both to himself and to society.

I remember well the impression made upon me when I was a little lad by the act of one of my chums. We had all been playing in a forbidden plantation, when the factor, a man with a very heavy hand, was sighted. Like rabbits, we all came out, crossed the road, and hid on the other side. All but one. He planted his brave little legs on the king's highway and waited for the enemy to come up. And I have never forgotten the shame I felt at our cowardice as with palpitating hearts we watched what would happen

to him, nor the queer feeling of respect and
reverence which his stand produced in my mind.
And what was it, after all, that made him stand ?
Just grit ! My brothers, if you and I only stood
for our principles and followed our conscience
as gamely as that little chap followed his schoolboy sense of honour and pluck, what a revolution
we should make in our immediate circle ! To
stand like that when you believe you are in the
right, to maintain, though it be alone, the cause
of righteousness when unrighteousness is popular
and men about you are bolting and failing, as
we ran away that day—that is to be of the tribe
of those who have printed their names deep upon
the world's memory. It is to be in the same
succession with Paul telling the Corinthians that
their judgment was a very small thing to him,
with Athanasius standing alone against the world,
or with Luther crying, " I can do no otherwise, so
help me God." It is to exhibit grit in the highest
sense, than which there is no more rare and
telling quality in human nature, none more had
in regard of men, and few, if any, more precious
in the sight of our Master Jesus Christ.

For, have you noticed how full the Gospels
are of praise of this very quality ? Do you remember the almost hopeless tone in which even
Jesus speaks of those who put their hands to the

plough, and then look back ?   Do you remember
that His ideal hearers are they which in an honest
and good heart having heard the Word, keep it
and bring forth fruit with patience ?   And,
finally, have you ever tried to make clear to yourselves that the only person to whom Christ
guarantees final salvation is " him that endureth
unto the end " ?

XXIX

THE EXCELLENCE OF THE ORDINARY

WHEN Naaman was ordered to bathe seven times in Jordan, he " was wroth and went away." For that reason we take him as our warning, because of his first refusal, and the grounds of it. He expected, he tells us, something very different, something quite exceptional and striking. But Elisha suggested such a very ordinary remedy that he was offended and turned away.

Our subject, then, is the excellence of things ordinary, and what we want to learn is that there is no surer way of cutting yourself off from healing and happiness, from the service and the knowledge of God, than by despising or esteeming lightly life's ordinary things.

Sometimes a preacher has declared what of all things he would like best to do. For my part, I should be content if I could persuade men of the riches that are hid in common vessels, of the glory of each common day, of the honour that attaches to the humblest and most ordinary duties. I should not envy my more gifted brother that he showed men God's glory in the heavens, if I could show them that same glory in the street, the market-place, and the home. For I know that, whatever else we men need, we need that, —to have religion expressed to us in terms of common life, to find a true and living link between our ordinary common duties and the fact of God and of His Christ.

So let me ask you to consider, first, that this Naaman-spirit largely explains the poverty of our service of the Lord, and the little joy we have in it. For some curious reason, when we think of serving the Lord, we never get beyond the idea of preaching or evangelising, or taking part in some of the work of the Christian Church. But that is not a tenth part of the service that is possible and that the Lord expects. It is not only the recruiting sergeant in a regiment who is serving his king and country. The other two hundred men, in the barracks, at drill, and engaged in all the other duties of a soldier's life, are serving as really as he. It is that ordinary service that we are so apt to overlook, and that Christ was at such pains to point out to us. He told the story of the Good Samaritan for no other reason. That kind-hearted soul was serving God as he went about his business better even than the priest or Levite were doing. Just to make sure that we should not overlook the commonest way of all of serving Him, He said that whatever we do unto one of the least of these His brethren, we do unto Him.

Not only so, but your daily calling is God's service. You are only a business man, you say. But does God not need business men ? Do you think that in His sight Jesus of Nazareth was wasting his time all those years He stood at the carpenter's bench ? If God gives you talents for Monday as well as Sunday, He needs your service on the one day as much as on the other.

In the Louvre at Paris, I have read, there is a famous painting by Murillo called " The Miracle of San Diego." Two noblemen and a priest, looking in to a kitchen, are struck with wonder to discover that all the kitchen-maids are angels. One is handling a water-pot, another a joint of meat, a third a basket of vegetables, and a fourth is tending the fire. The painter's vision is a great one, and he has a fine text for his sermon. But if angels may do that humble ordinary work as their service of God, why may not we ? And if God accepts it from angels, do you think He will refuse it from His children here on earth ?

Secondly, I suspect it is the Naaman-spirit that is very often at the bottom of our wish to

escape from a commonplace lot in life. There
are lives that are monotonous and depressing
enough, God knows; and means of alleviation
will have to be found for these. But I am not
speaking of them. I am speaking of your ordinary life and mine. We sometimes get sick of
what we are pleased to call the prose and common-
placeness of it—nothing but standing at a counter
or a desk, seeing clients, writing letters, catching
trains, or writing sermons. And, oh, we say,
for the wings of a dove! Now, that may mean
nothing more than that we need a holiday. But
it may also mean that we are making Naaman's
mistake, and it is a serious one. For it is not the
duties that are commonplace—no duty can be
that—it is that our eyes have drooped and closed,
and the glory of God's clean and ordinary blessing
of the day's work has been lost. Doves' wings
would not help matters much. It is eyes we
need, eyes to see our day's duty once again in
the light of the Father's will for us and need of
us, that we may go back to it like a soldier to
his post.

Thirdly, this Naaman-spirit blinds us to many
a revelation of God. I do not know many more
helpful principles in the sphere of Christian
doctrine than the discovery that God puts his
heavenly treasures in earthen vessels. That word

of the Apostle's illuminates in the most instructive fashion whole tracts of human life.

There are men, for example, who declare, "We have been told that God speaks to those who know Him and listen for His Voice, but we have never heard Him." Where have you listened, my brethren? Have you waited for some supernatural voice to be wafted to your ear? You will wait long for that. Not so, usually, does God speak to men. But perchance as you have listened to some brother's voice, your heart was stirred within you. That was God speaking to you. Maybe, as you read some worthy volume, a sentence in it struck fire upon your spirit and lit up a whole new avenue of desire or endeavour. That, again, was God. The book may have been quite commonplace, but there was heavenly treasure hidden in it for you. As Christ came unrecognised to the two on their way to Emmaus, and greatly comforted their hearts, so does He bring His comfort still, in the guise of a friend or a neighbour.

It is the greatest of all mistakes to stand gazing up to heaven expecting God's voice there, and not listening for it nearer at hand. He is about us on all sides, and, through the words of those we know, and the laughter of our children, and the peace of our homes, and the glory of His earth and sky and sea, is speaking to us all every day. But we often fail to hear, just because these channels are so ordinary.

We had no need to be told that God is great and awful and infinite. But that He is also little and near, can stoop to enter a lowly door, and lay His hands in blessing on little children, that He is willing to walk by our side through life's valley, sharing our burdens, and bearing our sins—that we needed to be told. And how have we learned it? Not because God has thundered it from His heaven. Not because that message was written by a blazing finger on the sky. It has come by what, in all reverence, we can only call an ordinary channel,—by a Man's speech, by a Man's love, by a Man's utter self-sacrifice. That is the last and greatest example of the use God makes of ordinary means. Do not let us belittle the common, the usual, and the human, as a vehicle of divinest revelation. For that, in the end, may mean to miss the glory of the Christ Himself.

XXX

UNCONSCIOUS INFLUENCE

THERE are two kinds of influence working in the world. There is the influence that is consciously exerted, when a man deliberately tries to persuade or compel another to a certain line of action.

But there is another kind of influence exerted unconsciously by every person on all with whom they come into contact. We have all met men and women in whose presence, altogether independent of what they may say, all that is best in us is somehow drawn to the top, with whom we feel it not only easy but natural to admire and covet whatsoever things are pure, lovely, and of good report. There are men and women, on the other hand, whose influence we feel no less strongly, but which we shrink from defining even to ourselves, though it is quite intelligibly summed up when we say it is exactly the reverse of that. Now, that kind of influence in one or other of these directions is exerted by everybody in a greater or less degree. It is independent of speech, and may even belie one's actual words. It is not the result of a deliberate intention. It is an atmosphere, a radiation which surrounds a character and affects others, not by the ordinary channels but in ways far more subtle and delicate, by the instincts, the intuitions, and all the most sensitive filaments of the soul. As the message springs off into the air from the Marconi mast in circles miles wide, so does character, for good or evil, send its invisible waves in all directions. Mark Rutherford in " Miriam's Schooling " tells us of an old man who, one Sunday afternoon, when he was twenty years of age, met a woman in a London street and looked her in the face. Neither he nor she stopped for an instant ; he looked, passed on, and never saw her again. He married and had children and grandchildren. But that woman's face never left him. A thousand times he appealed to it ; a thousand times did it sit in judgment upon him ; a thousand times did its sacred beauty in his eyes redeem him from evil. Yet he never knew her, and had never heard her speak !

This unconscious influence is infinitely more potent for good or evil than all that is ever done by taking thought. In Nature it is the constant and silent forces that are by far the greatest. The light that visits us so silently every morning

produces effects far more wide-reaching and beneficent than the lightning which splits the skies.

So is it in the realm of character. Words
may be misunderstood and actions may be mis-
interpreted, but the atmosphere—I do not know
what else to call it—the influence that radiates
from one honest soul transparently trying to
live up to the highest that he knows, touches
and blesses all those who come near him. We
all know men and women who rarely or never
have the phrases of religion on their lips and
yet their lives are telling on us, beyond all
that they ever suspect, for the very things that
religion stands for. If deliberate effort has re-
deemed its thousands, the aroma and fragrance
of a noble and godly life has inspired its tens of
thousands.

It is this sort of influence which reveals a man
better than anything else. There is no counter-
feiting the wireless influence of a truly good
life. It is what we really are that determines
the influence we exert. You may bend a piece
of soft iron horse-shoe shape, polish its ends and
paint it red, but that does not make it a magnet.
So, for his own ends, an evil-minded man may
observe all the conventions of society, and may
do many things that are reckoned unto him for
righteousness. But he cannot reverse his mag-

netism. He cannot make himself attract. That is
why the villains and hypocrites of history have
not exploited and deceived the world far more
than they have done. The instincts of men, and,
far more, the instincts of women and children,
have cried out in warning against them, even
when they seemed most plausible and sincere.
It is God's merciful provision to prevent the
hypocrite and the tricksters from inheriting the
earth.

The natural question—But am I to be held
responsible for the influence that I exert un-
wittingly upon others ? is already answered.
Yes, you are ! It is quite true that courts of
law take no cognisance of a criminal's influence
for evil, of the lives he may have blasted in his
progress. He has to answer simply for what he
has done. But there is a scrutiny of God at
once more just and more searching than any
human assize. And we cannot but be responsible
to Him for the influence we exert unconsciously
on others, since that is the one outward effect of
character about which there can be, in the long
run, no mistake.

It is just here that the whole reality and sig-
nificance of true religion becomes apparent.
The commission of Jesus to every disciple whose
life He has touched with His Spirit is, " Ye are the

light of the world." Now, what does a light do
but shine ? There is no thought of effort in the
figure. What Christ meant was that Christian
men and women, beyond all the good they try
to do (about which we are not speaking at all,
meantime), ought to BE such that their unconscious influence would tell constantly for righteousness and truth and honour and every quality and
interest of the Kingdom of Heaven.

This is an opportunity of service that is open
to the humblest disciple. We may not be able
to do much conscious good. But we can enshrine Christ's image in our hearts, and that will
tell. We have not authority or station, it may
be, to influence our fellows directly, but there is
a personal magnetism streaming constantly from
a sincere character and a consecrated life. The
truest help we can give our fellows in the long
run is to live our lives as nobly and purely as by
God's Grace we can. For no man, not even the
humblest and most self-distrustful of us, liveth
unto himself.

One of America's too-little-known poets, E. R.
Sill, has a haunting verse about life which may
fitly end our lesson :—

> "Forenoon and afternoon and night. Forenoon
> And afternoon and night. Forenoon and—what ?
> The empty song repeats itself. No more ?

Yea, that is life.   Make this forenoon sublime,
This afternoon a psalm, this night a prayer,
And Time is conquered and thy crown is won."

That is the secret of unconscious influence.
Make this forenoon sublime, this afternoon a
psalm, this night a prayer.

" The iron gate that leadeth
unto the city ; which opened to
them of its own accord."

(ACTS xii. 10.)

XXXI

THE IRON GATES OF LIFE

ONE of the stories in the Bible of which all our children are fond is the narrative of Peter's deliverance from prison by an angel, and of how when they were " past the first and second ward, they came unto the iron gate that leadeth unto the city; which opened to them of its own accord." But what are WE to make of this angel-story ? In our prosaic workaday life I am afraid we are not very sure about the angels, nor have very much room for them. But the strange thing is that our children are all quite sure. They believe in them, dear little hearts ! That is one of the things the Bible speaks about that they have no difficulty in receiving at all. It comes natural to them. You would have the greatest trouble in explaining to your three- or four-year-old, some of the doctrines of Scripture that are living and real to you ; but about the angels you would have none at all. It is more than likely indeed that instead of teaching, you would have to sit and be taught. And who knows but the

M

wonder and wisdom of a little child may be nearer
to God's vast and simple truth than all the guesses
of philosophers.

But, you say, this is a miracle and " miracles
do not happen." Well, I do not know what
your particular doctrine of miracles may be, but
I wish to suggest to you that just precisely this
sort of miracle is happening every day. Look
back a little in your own history and say, though
you have never caught the glint of an angel's
wing, if this thing has not also befallen you—the
gate, the barrier, the obstacle you were so much
afraid of, melted away apparently of its own
accord. Mark you, J do not say that always
happens. It does not. There are gates in life
we have to open for ourselves by hard effort and
perseverance. But of every one of us I am sure
it is true that we have in our time passed through
gates not a few that, to our great surprise, opened
unto us of their own accord.

I suggest to you, then, in the first place, that
this is true of the duties that lie in our path.
You have had something to do that troubled
you very much, a disagreeable interview, or some
responsible task. You contemplated some kindness and did not know how to go about it. Or
you felt compelled to go and make an apology
for something you had done amiss—perhaps one

of the hardest of the commoner sort of duties.
Whatever it was, there it lay in your way. It
had to be done. It would be cowardly to shirk
it, and yet you did not know how you were going
to manage. You bothered yourself about it all
the way up to it.

Yet, how many times has it happened that
that disagreeable duty proved on closer acquaint-
ance to be very much easier than you imagined ?
The interview you dreaded came off quite
pleasantly. The task you took upon yourself,
you discharged to the satisfaction of your friends.
Your offer of kindness paved its own way. Your
apology was received in the spirit in which it
was offered.

" I have an idea," says a recent writer, " that
the people which shortens its weapons wins its
battles. If you want to win, you must look your
enemy in the white of his eyes. You must
come to close grips with him." Yes, and when
you do, you will sometimes find that he is not an
enemy at all ! Whether the duty be some high
Christian one or only the ordinary everyday sort,
walk up to it ! It won't let you through before
that, but it may be that when you have faced it,
you will find it open of its own accord.

Then, in the second place, there is a large
amount of the trouble of life of which this is

certainly true. You remember that John Bunyan
tells how when Christian was nearing Palace
Beautiful he was dismayed to find that the entrance was guarded by two lions whose roaring
terrified him so that he started back and would
have fled. But Watchful, the porter, bade him
go boldly forward, keeping to the middle of the
path, and when he did so he found that the lions
were chained and could not reach him.

We have all made a similar mistake, and been
terrified by the roaring of chained lions. We
have been quite sure we could see trouble ahead
of us. We wore ourselves out in an agony of
apprehension beforehand. But when the time
came and brought us shrinking and fearful up
to the thing, behold, it was not there ! We
walked clean through what seemed to be sub-
stantial calamity !

There is one great message of the Gospel that
too few of us know, the message from God the
Father to all His children, Fear not ! There are
popular modern philosophies that have borrowed
it and are exploiting it as a new discovery. Fear
not, they say, for fear is a bad habit. Don't
allow yourself to be afraid of anything. But the
Bible says more than that. It says, " Fear not,
for I am with thee." And we need that addition.

Again I say, I do not wish to seem to speak

as if all life's troubles were of the sort that disappear when you approach them. But I do say that to every trouble without exception we may apply God's promise, " Fear not, for I am with thee " Do not let us forget, either, that our angel-story has another side to it. When Peter got back to his friends he found that, at the very time he was passing so easily through that hard gate, they had been praying for him. I wonder if he ever thought that that might be how he came by his angel and his quiet passage. Sometimes when our friend goes down to face his sorrow, we are at a loss what to say or do to comfort him. Does not our story suggest one way ? I like to think that it was the prayers of Peter's friends that oiled the hinges of that difficult gate of his, and set it so quietly open for his passage through.

There is another gate still, the last, the most feared gate of all, the gate of Death. We are all more or less terrified by the thought of it. We have said not a few Good-byes beside it—a dark and awesome portal.

We talked about the children, and of how they listen to the tale of Peter's angel. Will you let me tell you a story about this last gate of all, a children's story, taken from a children's book ?

You will make the application for yourselves. But here is the story : The railway into Edinburgh from the east goes through a long tunnel just before coming into the city. Now, there was a certain old lady, who lived in the country, who had a great dread of this long, dark tunnel, and so, though her friends laughed at her and tried to tease her out of it, she always used to get out at Abbeyhill, before the tunnel, and go into town by car. One day, when the train reached Abbeyhill, she was sleeping, and her friends did not wake her. So she passed through the tunnel she so much feared, in her sleep, and never knew it, and when she opened her eyes she was in the midst of the city.

XXXII

PROVIDENCE IN COMMON THINGS

JESUS, being on His way to Galilee, "must needs go through Samaria." It was the direct road there. And, tired with walking, when He came to the cool shade of a certain well, He sat down. That also was a perfectly natural thing to do. Ten minutes before, a woman of Samaria, engaged in her domestic duties, discovered that her water-pot was empty and started off to the well to fill it. Also a natural thing to do. These are ordinary details in an everyday picture. Yet in the picture there is more than in all the parts together. For the Power and the Grace of God are there. There came to that woman's heart that day, and to many others through her, something unmistakably divine and wonderful. Yet each of the stages in this incident was ordinary, common, natural. There was nothing in any of them to suggest God. Yet God was there. He was there from the beginning, in that ordinary "must needs go through Samaria." The truth I wish to set before you

is that if you would find God in your life, look at
its ordinary happenings, if you would discover
the supernatural, look for it behind the natural,
if you would realise the divine, do not overlook
the common. For the Lord always veils His
face when He speaks with men. The treasure
of heaven is always found in earthen vessels.
When you go, like the prophet's servant, to the
hill-top and anxiously scan the horizon round,
all that you will see is a cloud no bigger than
a man's hand. But the answer to the prophet's
prayer is in that.

We have all a hankering after the patently
miraculous. But Jesus was continually direct-
ing men's eyes in the other direction—to the
natural and the usual. It was in a blade of
grass, in a grain of mustard seed, in a man sowing a field, in a woman sweeping her house, in a
shepherd out on the hill after a stray sheep that
Jesus saw the Father, and showed Him to His
brethren. It was to the usual and the ordinary
that Jesus pointed as witnessing to the presence
of God.

Gather us together into church, and we shall
honestly sing the praise of the Guidance and
the Care of God ; but take us apart singly and
ask us to testify to even one act of Divine Providence in our own lives, and, except we have

already learned the secret, we are dumb. How comes that ? Are there no Providences nowadays ? What do you expect to find, my brother, when you look ? An angel with a drawn sword that keeps for you the way of life ? Your path made clear as by a lightning flash ? If it is that you seek, you must seek in vain. If that be Providence, then it is not in any ordinary life, nor yet in the life of Christ. For in the records of that life I find such things as this, that He must needs go through Samaria because that was the direct road to His destination. I find the faith of a whole nation made to depend upon that passage through Samaria. If there is an overruling hand anywhere, I am forced to admit that it is there. Yet there is nothing out of the common to be seen. The woman with the empty pitcher went to draw water and found the grace of God. If there is a Providence at all, surely it is there ? Aye, but where precisely ? Just in the empty pitcher. If you would see the divine in your life, it is for such things you must look.

In his younger days, A. B. Davidson had ambitions after a certain path in life, the entrance to which lay through a severe examination. He went up for it and failed. The consequence was that, by and by, he became a Professor in Edinburgh, and a most profound and helpful influence

in the lives of hundreds of his students. Davidson was turned into that path of usefulness, one
cannot doubt, by God. Yes, but how ? By a
heavenly messenger ? No, but by an examination paper !

" Are you coming to Drummond's meeting to-
night ? " one student asked another. He replied,
" I was not thinking of it, but I don't mind if I
do." In Drummond's meeting, as many another
man did, he found a Christ whom he could love
and serve, and the whole current of his life was
changed. Now, as he looks back upon that time,
he says, " It was not my friend's voice that asked
that question, it must have been the Voice of
God." Yet it was apparently as ordinary a
question as was asked in all the city that day.
Every link in the chain was natural, yet the chain
and the guidance were divine.

My brethren, be prepared to find that it is
always so. The finger of God is seen not so much
in any outward, eye-compelling intervention, as
in the quiet succession of apparently natural
events. These seem at the time to be mere
Samarias which must be passed through by a
necessity that has nothing divine about it, but
now and again even our dull human sight can
point to them as places where the ways parted,
a new purpose was born, and a new life began.

*" A sower went out to sow his
seed : and as he sowed, some
fell by the wayside."*

(LUKE viii. 5.)

XXXIII

WAYSIDE RELIGION

BY all different channels does God come near
to touch our lives—by hearing, by reading, in
thought, and through experience. These wander-
ing airs from some diviner clime, these seeds of
His sowing, we receive and react to in different
fashions. By some, they are welcomed and
cherished. They strike root and grow, and the
life exhibits the fruits of them, more and more.
The years as they pass bring increase of faith and
hope and love.

On other lives, too, the same influences are
acting, the same seeds are being sown. But
somehow the results are different. There is in
them no progress, no apparent growth in grace.
Religion, they have to confess, does not mean
much to them ; it is not so much an experience
as a few experiences, an occasional spasmodic
effort after holiness followed by a long season
of indifference and neglect, a brief reviving when
something does appeal to them, and, in the
strength of it, a vow made, prayers remembered,

187

the soul life cared for, for a little. But, by and by, the prayers are forgotten again, and the vow is not paid.

How does it come that similar influences produce such dissimilar results ? What is the trouble in lives so disappointing ? The seed is the same as in the other case ; it is good seed. May it not be the soil that is at fault ? " Some seeds," said Jesus in his great parable, " fell by the wayside," or, more correctly, " on the footpath." That was a hard surface, in summer as hard as a pavement, beaten like a stone by the constant passing of feet. Jesus said that on soil like that His seed cannot possibly grow.

There is a hardness of heart that is not so much natural as acquired. It is not the hardness that wrong-doing produces, but rather the impenetrability of the pathway on which there is much traffic. There is a danger, it would seem, of a man's spirit getting so hardened by the continual coming and going of daily routine and material interests and habits of life and work, that it becomes more like pavement than like kindly and receptive soil.

The traffic that beats the heart-soil hard may be quite legitimate. A man's spirit can become irresponsive to the things of God by absorption in interests which are quite lawful and innocent.

That is the serious aspect of this matter. We know what happens to the specialist unless he takes care. He becomes indifferent to what lies outside his own little province. It is an oft-quoted fact that Darwin, through allowing himself to become, as he said, a mere machine for the assimilation of facts of natural history, lost taste for poetry and music. One has heard of a famous mathematician who inquired what " Paradise Lost " was written to prove ! But it is possible to incur the specialist's danger without actually being one. You can make a speciality of your business, or your pleasure, or your home, or all of these together. Your mind can be so filled with them that there is room for little else. Worthy and proper as these are, the constant tramp in that groove can so dull and deaden a man's response to other interests, even those of his spirit in its relation to God, that that side of his nature grows callous and hard.

But how, it may be said, is one to prevent that ? The answer, of course, is that, as it is habit that works this evil, so it is habit that cures it or avoids it. A man is more than a foot-path. He can do things for himself. And more, he can let God do things in him. It is a dead-sure fact that if we fail to cultivate our soul life, and use the means to this end that God has given us, we shall grow irresponsive, indifferent, and finally hard.   But it is just as certain that the way is open backwards.   Your plant will die if you forget to water it.   But when you see it drooping, you have the means of cure at hand, provided it be not actually dead.   Begin and water it again, and it will revive.   We are being told in these days many wonderful things about the power of habit—and habit, for us, just means the way ordained by God.   We are being reminded of the mighty power that lies in the cumulative influence of small and constant forces.   You can set a great mass of a pendulum swinging by tapping it with a cork suspended by a thread, if only you tap steadily and patiently.   Even so, habit can build up again what disuse has partly taken away.   Darwin said that if he had been wise, he should have given a few minutes every day to poetry and music.   That, he said, would have kept his literary and musical soul alive.   And so it would.   If he had begun, indeed, after he made the discovery of his loss, it would not have been too late.

The antidote to wayside hardness is just a few minutes every day, in the interests of one's highest life, with God, in the Spirit-company of Jesus Christ.   Soul life, spiritual life, is God's gift to begin with.   But it needs culture and tending, and He has provided means for that. We must do the rest. There are blessings that prayer brings us. But to receive them we must ourselves practise prayer. He has given us His Word. But we must read it and follow it. He has many voices for us in the world of Nature and experience, in the realms of Art and Literature and Science, but we must listen for them, look for them, attend to them.

They say that in certain valleys in Switzerland, the roads are kept open in winter because every house and hamlet in the valley sends its one or two every Sunday to church. So we keep open the ways that lead to God by the constant traffic along them of our thoughts and prayers, by daily betaking ourselves out of the dust of the day's duty to where we know He is to be found.

It is just here that so many orthodox people are sadly heretical in practice. They honour the Grace of God, believing that salvation is only in Him. But they forget that constant and habitual efforts on their part are called for too. Religion means little more than the germ of a godly life with some people because they have not realised that they must bestow care and attention upon it if it is to grow. It is true that it is God who giveth the farmer his increase, yet it is he who must break up his fallow ground and prevent it from getting hard. Many good people have a strange dislike to that precept which bids us "work out our own salvation because it is God that worketh in us." But it was Paul who said that, and he is not the man to belittle the grace of God. The words he uses for the Christian life, indeed, like "fight," "wrestle," and "race," are in themselves a rebuke to that ignorance that would leave everything to God to do. There is a place, and a big place for culture, education, habit, effort, in all genuine spiritual life. Brother Lawrence called his famous book "The Practice of the Presence of God"—practice, a verb of effort, a word implying exercise again and again. If the traffic of the busy days is not to harden our hearts to the seeds of God's sowing, we must find a place in our idea of religion for its "active" verbs.

" And let fall also some of the
handfuls of purpose for her."
(RUTH ii. 16.)

XXXIV

HANDFULS, OF PURPOSE

" IF we wish a model of a kindly heart," says
some one of the Book of Ruth, " let us stop at
Boaz." We shall stop at Boaz, then, for kindness
is a lesson which we all need to learn. It takes
all our care and all the grace of God, even when
we have remembered to be zealous and upright
and devout, to keep us from forgetting also to be
kind. And I do not think we realise as often as
we should, that, when we have forgotten that,
we have forgotten everything.

" Now, when Ruth had risen up to glean,
Boaz commanded his young men saying, ' Let
her glean even among the sheaves. And let fall
also some of the handfuls of purpose for her, and
leave them that she may glean them, and rebuke
her not.' " Ruth had come down in the world.
Once she had been well off, but now for the sake
of her dead love she had taken Naomi's poverty
voluntarily upon her, and must swallow her pride
and go out to glean with other poor folk. Now,
suppose Boaz had come up to her with an armful

N   193 of corn, and said, " Here, woman, here is a little extra for you, because we are all sorry for you," I question if, for all her love, this young Moabite widow would have suffered a charity so stark as that. Ruth was one of those people whom it is difficult to help. So Boaz took a roundabout. He actually instructed his workers to leave some extra handfuls where she gleaned, that she might gather a good store, and not be put to shame. He was thinking of Ruth's feelings, you see !

And the Bible, which has so much to tell us about God and His Christ and the way of salvation, wastes one whole precious chapter telling us how, on a harvest field of long ago, a farmer went a roundabout to save a poor woman's face ! Why should that be ? I think it must be because it is so vital and important that we should learn how to be kind, that, even if He should tell us less about Himself and less about heaven, God would not have that chapter omitted from His Book.

That unkindness hurts, nobody needs to be told. But that kindness may hurt too, sometimes, when it is done in the wrong way, we all need to remember. It is a strange thing that you may approach people with the very best intentions in the world of helping them, and make them feel for all that, as if they had received a blow in the face.   There is an art, in fact, in being kind, and, like every other art, it concerns itself with the small details.   It was kind of Boaz to wish to help Ruth, especially since her circumstances were peculiar, but it was the very high art of kindness for him to think how he could help her in the way that would be most agreeable to her.   It is in the art of being kind that we oftenest fail.   You may say, about any of the ordinarily and humanly kind things that we all have the chance to do every day, that the great thing is that we do them.   In all truth, that is a great thing.   But there is a greater thing still, and that is how we do them.   It may be just the tiniest trick of manner or of speech, just the difference of a smile or a silence in the wrong place that determines whether your offering is an acceptable gift, gratefully received, or a burdensome favour which your neighbour would refuse if she dared.   It may be a very little thing which determines how she shall feel about it, but the whole art of being kind lies just in that little thing.

We have all the chance to discover this for ourselves, for there are none of us so independent that we have not, at some time or other, to receive favours or help from our friends.   We know the difference between receiving a kindness that we are simply grateful for, and one that growls and grumbles in the memory like an aching tooth. Yet if we were asked to point out the blunder, we should have to speak of very little things. It was something in his look, something he said or did not say, one word that slipped out before he noticed it—it was something little, anyway. Now, we are far on the way to learn the art of being kind when we remember that those whom we have the privilege of helping have precisely the same feelings as ourselves. There is a short name for that—Sympathy. The art of being kind lies, firstly, and secondly, and thirdly, in being sympathetic.

" Some handfuls." It is a little thing to devote a chapter of God's Word to. Only a few extra handfuls of corn ! But it made a poor woman happy that day. And it stands as a reminder that happiness is very often just a matter of small things. Chesterton, in his book on Browning, says, " Browning had one great requirement of a poet. He was not difficult to please." Even though we have no gift of utterance, we are all poets in that sense. It does not take much to make us happy. Happiness is that which happens to us—a beam of sunlight falling on our face, a smile from some one we love, some little token of a friend's good-will, the impression our neigh-

bour conveys that he is glad to see us. Joy, it
has been said, is the gift of God, but happiness
may be a man's gift to his brother. The contribution of Jesus to the solving of the problem
of living, on its everyday plane at least, is just
that we are here to add to the happiness of others
in the little world in which we live.

It is not as if it were a great task. It is because
of the very littleness of it that we so often fail.
It is only now and then that a home is wrecked
by gross unkindness or deliberate cruelty. But
a woefully common thing it is that our homes
are made a little less happy than they might be,
just because in the contributions which you and
I make to home's happiness, we forget the small
change. We pay the pounds and shillings of
affection, but we forget the pence. We make
the sacrifice, but we forget to smile. We live for
them, and work for them, but we do not hold in
the hasty snap of temper. We forget the pence.
And the day has come to many a man when he
would have given everything he possessed to
have had more entries in that pence column—
the day when our loved ones pass beyond our
reach. God knows we would have undertaken
any sacrifice for his sake. But a smile would
have made him happy that day, and we frowned.
A caressing touch and an easy cheerful word

would have made all the difference to her, on a certain day that we remember. But the word and the touch are not recorded in the column of Love's little things. There was that service that she asked from us, and that we rendered, but we spoilt it, for we did it with " a bad grace." No, we cannot say it too often, the art of making happy those whom we love is an art that takes account of the smallest things.

It is not otherwise outside of home. Let us get rid of our stupid contempt for details in the great business of Christian living. There is nothing small that ministers to the happiness of a single soul.

According to the genealogy given in the Gospels, Boaz was an ancestor of the Saviour of the world —Boaz whose only claim to remembrance is that he took the trouble not only to be kind, but to be kind in the kindest possible way, Boaz who had the grace to see that the art of making happy is concerned not only with sheaves but with handfuls. We want to remember that. Boaz stands for the art of being kind. And spiritually as well as genealogically, the line of Boaz is the line of Jesus Christ.

" And it came to pass when the minstrel played, that the hand of the Lord came upon him."

(2 KINGS iii. 15.)

XXXV .

OUR MINSTRELS

ONCE, when Elisha wanted to know the Lord's will, he asked that a minstrel from the camp should be brought to him. " And it came to pass, when the minstrel played, that the hand of the Lord came upon Elisha." It looks a very ordinary means of grace. It seems strange that God should speak to any man through such a channel. But the truth is that we, too, are indebted, oftener than we perhaps realise, to agencies and instruments, as material and unlikely as Elisha's minstrel, for effects and an inspiration as truly divine.

There was a time in Ruskin's life, one of his interpreters tell us, when the sense of life's sins and sorrows and wrongs swept over his heart with the might of a destroying storm. The pen dropped from his hand, and hope departed from his heart. One day, crossing the Square of St Mark's at Venice, he saw the Cathedral rising like a vision out of the ground, " its front one vast forest of clustered columns, upon which rested domes glorious enough to have been let down from heaven." As he lingered there, and by-and-by stepped inside, slowly the fever passed from his heart and the fret from his mind. In the silence and peace of that vast architecture, he found healing for life's hurt. It said something to him that it might not have said to you and me. It was his minstrel, that thing of stone and lime !

Are there not many happenings in our lives that echo to that experience ? I cannot describe them to you, for of course I only know my own. But have you not felt the hand of the Lord upon you, when you listened to the wind sighing among heather, or watched the sea break on a lonely shore, or heard a hill-bird call in the night ? There are books we read, and poems we love, and music that our soul delights in, that have the strange power of saying to us far more than the mere words or melody can express. There is comfort in them for our hour of sorrow, a new hope for us when we are weak, far beyond what the authors ever put there. We turn to them again and again, not for what they are in themselves— for others to whom we have shown them may think them nothing out of the common—but for the thoughts and the spirit they have the power to call up in us. They are our minstrels, and the hand of the Lord is on us as they play. And that is all one can say about it.

We need not be distressed if they are peculiar to ourselves. Possibly there were others around who heard Elisha's minstrel play, but the hand of the Lord was not on them the while.

Two of Wordsworth's most quoted lines are these :—

> " To me the meanest flower that blows can give
> Thoughts that do often lie too deep for tears."

There are some of us who think we know what the poet meant when he wrote that. But Arnold of Rugby says of them, " There is something in the lines of a morbid feeling. Life is not long enough for us to take such intense interest in objects themselves so little." Does that mean that Wordsworth and those who feel with him are wrong ? No, but only that there is a divine variety in the channels through which man comes on thoughts of God and goodness. The flower that spoke to the poet had no message for his friend and neighbour Arnold. And so the book that contains the very portrait of Jesus Christ for me, may seem to my friend dull and uninteresting. What helps you to realise the presence and the love and the holiness of God may be only a hindrance to your neighbour.

In his ordinary life there are doubtless visible
things and places that speak to him of God,
where you and I, perhaps, get no such message.
We only make a mistake, and we make it far too
often, when we are tempted to deny that our
brother's minstrel can speak to him of God because
his music sounds only earthly in our ears. From
some village pump one draws water in a pitcher,
another in a cup, and a third fills a vase for
flowers. And the vessels are all different, but,
my brothers, the water is the same !

> "O thou who would'st unity make through strife,
> Canst thou fit that sign to the Water of Life ? "

What does it mean that besides what we call
the ordinary means of grace, there should be,
in all our lives, happenings, people, places, things
that have the strange power of calling our thoughts
Godwards and to His Truth ? What can it
mean but that in our common lives, and from
the things that we see and hear every day, God
can and does speak to us as really as He speaks
through His Church ? It is they who love Him
best, and whose lives are fullest of His Spirit,
who hear Him thus the oftenest ; but, at times,
the very dullest of us can catch, in the strains of
some earthly minstrel, a meaning greater and
diviner than the player knows ; at times, even

our vision pierces the visible to behold the hem of the garment of the Lord. To the eyes of Jesus, His material life from end to end was full of memorials of the Father. He saw Him in the flowers of the field. He heard Him in the night wind sighing among the tree tops. In the little red-cheeked boy who ran in and out among their feet, the listeners might see but a village bairn, but to Jesus, as He caught him up and set him in the midst, he was the very embodiment, in his trust and artlessness, of that heart kingdom which He came to found. And in proportion as our hearts are touched with His Spirit, so shall we also see and hear. If our lives were purer and our devotion more real, our life would be fuller of these minstrels of God, and we should find richer treasure even in the vessels of earth. For it is the listener's heart that makes the minstrel's message.

" *An evil beast hath devoured
him ; Joseph is without doubt
rent in pieces.*"

(Genesis xxxvii. 33)

XXXVI

IN PARALLEL COLUMNS

At the end of the year, the man with a bank
account gets all his used cheques returned in a
bundle. What an instructive thing it would be
if we could get all our fears and apprehensions
during the year returned to us in the same fashion,
so that we could see how many of them had been
honoured, how many of them had come true !
Or, to change the figure, suppose that, after a
year of life, we could read it like a history in
parallel columns, one for fears and one for facts,
so that at any moment we could see what we
thought or feared about a certain interest, and
then, by referring to the other column, could find
out what had really been happening at that time,
what a revelation that would be, and what a
lesson for us all !

Of course, we should also find that joys we
expected turned out sorrows, that anxieties that
haunted us were too true prophets of trouble.
But I want, if I can, to persuade you that in a
normal experience these are the exceptions, and

that our duty to God is to treat them so, and not, as we so often do, as the things to be most surely looked for. I want to remind you how often in our apprehensive fashion we have tried to forecast the future or even to interpret the present, and been hopelessly and blessedly wide of the mark.

The history in parallel columns is, alas! not possible, but in the Bible we have the story of other lives written out so that we can see the end from the beginning, and in a well-known incident from the life of Jacob we have a striking instance of how God delights to disappoint man's fears. His beloved son Joseph is away on a journey, and a blood-stained coat is brought to the father. The conclusion is swift and bitter. Joseph has fallen a prey to some wild beast! But turn to the parallel column of Scripture, and do we find Joseph's bones bleaching beside some animal's den? No, we find Joseph himself on his way to Egypt, where by and by he reigns as a prince and succours the father who is mourning him as dead.

You will point out, of course, that Jacob's conclusion was perfectly natural under the circumstances. Joseph was absent, there was the story of the other sons, and here was the coat all

stained with blood. You can't blame Jacob for
making the inference he did.

I am not blaming him. I want you to admit
fully that the conclusion on the evidence before
him was perfectly natural, because I am going
to remind you, next, that it was wrong! It
was a fear which from Jacob's point of view
looked as certain as could be, and yet it proved
groundless.

What I marvel at, in myself and others, is
that "natural conclusion" should almost always
be synonymous with "worst possible conclusion."
There are people who never board a train but
they have a clear vision of the possibility of an
accident before they reach the end of their
journey, who never see a telegraph boy come in
at their gate but they suspect evil news. And
we say that is natural. But the point I wish
to make is—Why should not the natural conclusion be the most hopeful one? Why, when
we piece together the fragments of the puzzle
of what is coming, as the child fits his blocks
together to make a picture, why should it be
natural to turn the black side uppermost? Some
chance word we have had repeated to us by a
busybody, which one we deemed our friend has
said behind our back, fills us with bitter thoughts
and makes us rail against false friends. But this

puzzle block has its white side—the words may be inaccurate, or may be capable of another explanation. There is at least the faithfulness of a lifetime to put into the other scale. But no ! we turn the thing black side up and have eyes for no other aspect than that. That may be natural, but it is not Christian.

The man who has accepted the view of God and the world which Jesus has enshrined in His life and teaching, ought to believe that the bright side is the right side. It was not a pagan philosopher, but our Lord Himself who found this faith, proved it, and handed it down to you and me—" Sufficient unto the day is the evil thereof."

In his life already, Jacob had seen very black clouds break in blessings on his head. He was very lonely and full of fears, for example, when he lay down in Bethel, yet events proved that he had made his bed that night very near to the gates of heaven. It was a black lookout for him when Esau was hastening to meet him with four hundred men, but how happily the gloom broke up in the gladness of reconciliation !

How many times, my brother, have you foreseen evil in store for you and it did not come ? Surely the most unfortunate of us can say that there has been more sunshine than shadow in our lives ?

" There are nettles everywhere,
But tall, green grasses are more common still ;
The blue of heaven is larger than the cloud."

Seeing that our fears have been disappointed
so often, is it not time for us now to look at life
from the other point of view, and instead of cower-
ing from the anticipated blow, go forth with hopeful heart to welcome the blessing ?　I like these
lines of Aldrich's because I believe they are true
to the Spirit of Christ :

" I'll not confer with sorrow
Till to-morrow.
But Joy shall have her way
This very day."

Early in his life, God had made Jacob quite
sure that He meant good by him, and only good.
He had received a promise, as he believed, that
he was under the watchful guardianship of God.
I can imagine that, when Jacob found out the
truth in the matter of Joseph, he was moved
to declare that he might have been more hopeful,
that he need not have been so quick to suspect
evil.　Is it going beyond the bounds of fitness
to imagine what God thought ?　In spite of all
He had done for Jacob, and was planning to do
still, was He likely to be pleased that Jacob should
be so quick to take sides with appearances against
Him ?

You and I believe, on the testimony of Jesus, in the Fatherhood of God. With some of us it is perhaps the central pillar of our creed. Try, then, to eke out your conception of what that means, as Christ invited us to do, by reading into it your own ideas of Fatherhood. Suppose that your son, to whom you had given abundant proof of your affection, went about fearing constantly that you purposed to do him some hurt, would you not, at least, be disappointed? And is not that the fashion in which many of us treat God? You would be much better pleased if your son persisted in believing, in spite of all appearances, that you had something good in store for him, even when it was not what he expected. Does not God desire that we should honour Him with the same confidence? To suffer an evil that has not yet come, to shoulder a burden that He has not as yet laid upon us—is not that to do a dishonour to the Love of God?

The conclusion of the matter then was that Jacob was mistaken and Joseph was not dead. Bad as the case seemed, the bright side turned out the right side after all. God was kinder to Jacob than he imagined. He had to change his view, and change it penitently before God.

The hopeful outlook for which I am pleading, the optimism which Christ would teach us, may

o

sometimes have to change its view too, though not so often as the other. But it does not need to confess and ask God's forgiveness when it changes. Shall God be angry that you looked for sunshine, and, in His wisdom, He appointed cloud? Nay indeed, for what you expect from God is your little measure of what He is to you; and poor and distorted as the mirror may be, the Father will not be displeased that the Face it reflects seems gracious.

I know right well that we cannot argue one another into that chronic optimism which is just a braver faith in God. We can never prove that it is justified, save by adopting it. Yet, short of that, there is a homely little test that carries its own weight with it. Ask yourself who are the men and women you know who are not only the happiest themselves, but seem to have the gift of shedding gladness like a fragrance about them, wherever they go. Is it not those who have learned to look for the bright and hopeful side of everything, who live, as the saying goes, on the sunny side of the street? If that be true, ought not you also to " flit " to that side?

XXXVII

A SIN WITHOUT A NAME

ONE of the Seven Deadly Sins, according to the mediæval moralists, bears a name which will be perfectly strange to most of you. Did you ever hear of the sin of Accidie ? The preachers of the Middle Ages spoke much of it. You will find it given a dreadful doom in Dante's "Inferno." Yet the word has passed completely out of use. But has the thing itself disappeared ? I think not, and that is why I want to speak about it.

In the " Spirit of Discipline " by the late Bishop Paget, there is the best-known modern description of this sin, from which we learn that Accidie is heaviness, gloom, coldness, sullenness, and desultory sloth in work or spiritual privilege, joylessness, and thanklessness. It is the mood of days when we " can't be bothered," when we have no joy in life, when the work we have begun looks stale and poor and unattractive like the scenery on an empty stage, seen by daylight, when, without anything really to complain of, nothing stirs in us so readily as a complaint or a grumble. Is that purely mediæval, think you ?

God knows there are sorrows enough in the world that are real—sorrow, too, that, humbly and bravely borne, yieldeth a peaceable fruit, but the sorrow that one makes, the sorrow that is part indolence of will, and part irritation and discontent, the " sorrow of the world," as the Apostle calls it, that sorrow, he says, " worketh death." Depression is often only another name for a weak, unmanly giving-in. It disappears when the spirit within rises up and defies it. Sometimes just to see a heroic soul combating his moods, and gaily denying them, sends a glow of emulation into the most timorous of us, and drives us back to our conflicts with a surge of new valour in our hearts. It is a shame and a sin, we say to ourselves, for anyone to be sad and hopeless who has once believed in God. Accidie is ultimately cowardice. If we must be beaten, my brothers, let us be beaten fighting, hoping, striving. " Why art thou cast down, O my soul, and why art thou disquieted in me ? Hope thou in God."

But what, says Accidie, is the use of trying to be good ? Isn't it Might that is Right when all is said and done ? Isn't it the one who can sink his convictions, and pare the edges off his principles on occasion, that gets along, on the whole, most comfortably ?

By some means or other, the man who is laps-ing into that attitude must be whipped and stung out of it into taking the road again, or, like those who lie down in a snowstorm, he will perish.   A man is done for who has lost faith in his own capacity to be what God meant him, and Christ invites him, to become.   There is always a new chance in God's mercy for him who is willing to try again.   In this affair of outposts which we call life, the Christian soldier must be willing to stake all he has on his highest ideals being proved true in the end of the day. It may at times look otherwise, for there is discipline in it.   But let him, having taken his side, stick to it, believe in God and himself, in truth and righteousness and purity and love, believe in the presence and help of his Lord, and never, while he has breath in his body, take lower ground.

The outcome of a peevish despondency re-garding the highest things is inevitably a slack-ening of moral effort.   It is here that Accidie has its characteristic fruit.   Accidie comes to be the sin of slackness.   And a sin with which we are far too gentle.

Part of the subtlety of Accidie is that it is

often as much bodily as spiritual. Conditions of health, overwork, and what not are frequently contributing causes. That fact ought to be borne patiently and charitably in mind when we are dealing with the short-comings of others. It is true wisdom, however, to beware of extending such charity to any symptoms of Accidie in ourselves. Probably, indeed, most of us need to cultivate a healthier contempt for our own bodies and their minor disabilities and protests. While judging our fellows in all gentleness, what you and I need to insist on to ourselves is that what makes us on some days so singularly unpleasant to others and to ourselves, is not the East wind, nor yet dyspepsia, nor overwork, but a subtle and complex trouble of mind and spirit which a little more courage and resolution, and a little less tender dealing with ourselves would effectually dispel.

In Sir Walter Scott's Journal we find this entry : " I am very ill to-day with rheumatic headache, and a still more vile hypochondriacal affection which fills my head with pain, my heart with sadness, and my eyes with tears. I worked therefore and endured all this forenoon." Brave soul! Does it not make us ashamed of what we have shirked, on the plea of some minor bodily discomfort ? I came across a picture of a very heroic soul recently. I wonder if you could guess who this is? " Little, thin, shockheaded, undignified in appearance, always sick when afloat, racked by a terrible cough, tormented with fever and pains, crippled, with one eye, and one arm." Who was that ? A man, you would say, who should be in the hospital ! Yet that was the sailor who made Britain supreme at sea. It is a description of Horatio, Lord Nelson.

The older writers are quite clear on the point that, though Accidie may be partly physical in its origin, its ultimate source is in the Will, and it is there, therefore, that the remedy is to be applied. A man can, if he choose, shake himself out of that gloom for which there is no real reason, and he ought to do so, just as he ought to resist the Devil. One of the very best ways of encouraging him to do that, is to procure for him a near-hand sight of something of the real sorrow and pain and sadness that there is in the world and all around him. Let him help somebody who is in real distress, and the hole out of which he pulls his friend will be the grave in which he buries his own cherished gloom. This was Keble's cure for melancholy—" When you feel yourself overpowered," he said, " the best way is to go out and do something kind to some one or other."

Did not Job himself find that his " captivity was turned when he prayed for his friend ? "

Moreover, when the mood of Accidie is heavy on one, and all high effort or purpose seems impossible, it is always a good plan to do something, even though it be merely routine and mechanical. " When we seem poorest and least spiritual," says Paget, " when the glow of thankfulness seems to have died quite away, at least we can go on with the comparatively featureless bits of work, the mechanisms of life, the tasks which may be almost as well done then as ever." Benson in " A Thread of Gold " puts the same truth more picturesquely. " If one has the courage and the good sense, when in a melancholy mood, to engage in some piece of practical work, it is wonderful how one can distract that great beast which, left to itself, crops and munches the tender herbage of the spirit."

Help somebody is one good rule. Do something, though it be mere hackwork, is another. But, last and best, for overcoming the sin of Accidie, remember, remember that God in all probability did not give you life and being in this world of His, merely that you should have a comfortable and easy time. Remember, too, that at your baptism and your first Communion you were sworn to be a soldier of Christ, and it is not soldierly to skulk. Christ's call to you to be your best in His strength and to follow Him overrides all questions of how you may feel. A well-known preacher has suggested what Christ's answer might be to the man who protests that he cannot serve in this or that way or at this particular time because he feels depressed and not himself. He imagines that Jesus would say, " What is that to thee ? Follow thou Me." It is a wise imagining, for that is exactly the word that Accidie needs.

" Toward Jerusalem."
(DANIEL vi. 10.)
" Toward Sodom."
(GENESIS xiii. 12.)

XXXVIII

TOWARD

IN the life of Daniel and in that of Lot there is
a " note of direction " which is very significant.
Daniel opened his windows *toward* Jerusalem,
and Lot pitched his tent *toward* Sodom. In these
contrasted directions, the life-stories of the two
men are told in brief.

Every character has one supreme direction.
There is no gainsaying that, I imagine. We
have all many interests in life. There are many
directions in which we develop our original
holding. We are keen on this, that, or the other
thing. But on analysis it must be found that
one of these is supreme. When there is a conflict
of interests, there are some that we allow to go
to the wall.

It was as much Daniel's wish as it would have
been yours or mine to keep out of the lions' den
and to stand well with the king. But he saw
clearly that to follow that direction would be for
him to be false to his God. There, then, were
two competing motives. He had to elect one to

the supreme place. And he had done it when he opened his windows toward Jerusalem in the sight of the whole town.

Lot, likewise, knew what Sodom was. There was the talk of the countryside about Sodom's reputation, and there was a voice of God within his own heart. On the other hand were the man's keen commercial instincts and his love of money. He had to elect one of these directions to be the supreme one. And he had made his choice when he pitched his tent toward Sodom. There is a direction in life which a man makes supreme. It can be what he likes. It may be Daniel's, or Lot's, or countless others besides. But a chief and controlling direction every man must have, every man actually has. The question is—What is it? Toward what?

For it is direction that is the only true and just test of character. That there are other tests we all know, and many of us have winced under them. The matter-of-fact world has its test for all religious profession. Of course, it is practical. " Let us see what they do," it says. And too often it has cause to point its finger in scorn at the doings which it can see. The critic, both without us and within us, asks for facts, and there they are, some of them shameful, dishonouring, damning facts! Now, I do not for one moment seek to underrate the value of that standard.   But I want you to know that there is a fairer test than that, Heaven's test.   The world asks, " What does the man do ? "   But Heaven asks, " What was he trying to do ?   What is the main set and purpose of his life ? "   By a blamable error in navigation the ship may run out of her course, or a tempest may drive her headlong before it. But the question at last comes to be—What port was the captain trying to reach ?

It is the easiest thing in the world to pick faults in the life of the Christian man or woman. Peter once denied his Lord with curses.   But is there no difference between his cowardice, sad and shameful as it was, and the cold, calculating spite of the Chief Priests who did Jesus to death ? Peter's denial was not a fair sample of his attitude toward the Master.   We say of a river that it flows south, if that is its main direction, even though for a little it may bend some other way. Peter turned shamefully north in his course for a while, but the river of his love was, over all, southwards and Christ-wards for all that.   And Christ knew it.   He always knows it.   Even from the legitimate discipline of conscience and the sneers of his friends, a man feels that there is an appeal to Christ Himself, who knows.   We have wandered and turned aside, but Christ knows

whether we love Him or not, whether we are
really trying to follow Him or not.

You remember how Christian and his friend
Pliable in the " Pilgrim's Progress " fell into the
Slough of Despond together, and got plentifully
bemired in consequence ? Bunyan's whole
passage is a masterpiece, but there is one touch
in it that is unsurpassed. After describing how
Pliable turns tail and leaves Christian, Bunyan
goes on : " Wherefore Christian was left to
tumble in the Slough of Despond alone, but still
he endeavoured to struggle to that side that was
furthest from his own house and next to the
wicket gate." There you have the test of direction, met and passed ! The side next the wicket
gate ! Ah, my brothers, there is no promise that
we shall escape the pitfalls and the accidents even
though we follow the light from Heaven, but if
only we struggle toward the far side of the bog,
if, miry as we are, we clamber forward to the
side nearest to the gate of God, it surely will be
well with us in the end. For it is not his falls
that altogether determine whether a man be a
true Christian pilgrim or not. It is the side he
makes for out of the mire.

I have sometimes imagined to myself another
ending to the Parable of the Prodigal Son. I
have seemed to see the wanderer come limping

and weary all those sorrowful miles back on the way home. But night fell as he was getting in among the old landmarks, and the cold chilled him, and his strength was nearly spent. Yet he struggled bravely on till he came to the road-end that turned up for home, but there he had to give in. There he fell down at last, and lay, face forward, with his arms outstretched, as if he would have gone farther if he could. There the hired servants found him in the morning, cold and stiff and dead. When they brought the old man out, do you think he turned away because the confession had not been spoken? Ah, no. He read in those outstretched arms what it was the wanderer had tried to say. And with tears in his eyes and a great gladness in his heart, he said, "It is my son, come home." It is with a judgment and a love like that we have to do. A love that looks more at what we aim at than at what we reach. A Master who generously counts for service what we should have liked to do. A Father who looks, not at the fall only, but at the road we were travelling on when we fell.

" I will bless thee, . . . and
thou shalt be a blessing."
(GENESIS XII. 2.)

XXXIX

CONTAGIOUS BLESSINGS

SOME one has said that this would be a very much happier and better world if God had just thought of making health contagious rather than disease. As a matter of fact, God has thought of that, and decreed it. Health is contagious rather than disease in the long run. God has organised His world on such lines that it is the good and helpful and beautiful that tend to grow and flourish, and all that is hurtful, base, and cruel to die out and disappear. When you take short views, this, I admit, seems to be contradicted by the facts of experience ; but when you embrace in your outlook a sufficiently long space of time, it stands proved and true. Match a good thing against a better, and see which will spread faster. Into a world where all the printing was done by hand—to use an apt illustration of Newell D. Hillis's—introduce a steam printing-press, and what happens ? The better method spreads like a contagion. When an improved tool is invented, everybody gets it. When a

more rapid and effective method of manufacture
is discovered, new machines are ordered everywhere, and the old ones "scrapped." So it is
in every sphere. Good is contagious, spreads
faster than what is less good.

In the realm of the spiritual the same holds
true. The Christ-like character tends to spread
and perpetuate itself in a community by a
stronger and surer necessity than the debased
and vicious type. There is really no question
as to the ultimate triumph of Christ and all that
He stands for, in the world, because He stands for
the Best, for all that men in their right moments
must love, and honour, and worship. In this
world of God's the Best wins and spreads by a
slow but sure contagion of its own. Those whom
God blesses become blessers in their turn.

For all of us common folk there is a great in-
centive in that truth. If all the good that is
done in the world were the result of arguing and
speaking and preaching, what slow progress
would be made ! If only those who were gifted
in speech could be witnesses for Christ, what a
small number of servants He would have !
But it is not so. The sincere, earnest, Christ-like
life is a tremendously influential thing of itself.
If we cannot speak we can at least try to live.
If we cannot prove or commend the Best by our

eloquence, we can do something by following it ourselves, and so maybe commend it by our lives.

By our cheerfulness, for one thing. Let us determine for Christ's sake that as far as in us lies, we shall face life with a smile, because we believe that life means good in the end, and means God. Let us resolve that we shall keep our troubles to ourselves, and our weather eye lifting for trouble's danger signals in other lives, when a kind word or a cheerful greeting may be of service. It's a very simple way of doing good, but a very effective one. For cheerfulness is a contagious thing, and " a heart at leisure from itself " can bless a whole community.

By fighting the good fight of faith bravely ourselves—for another thing. Erasmus has a story of how a company riding to Richmond were all persuaded to believe they had seen a great portent in the sky, because one of the party, for a joke, declared that he saw it, and kept repeating what it looked like. If even an imagined vision be so powerful as that, how much more the faith of one who really sees, and cleaves to what the inward eye reveals. Faith begets faith. Stand up boldly for what you believe, and the disheartened and faithless will gather to your side.

But chiefly perhaps we commend our belief by our steadfastness. There is no finer witness

P

for the truth of the Christian religion than a Christian who is dead straight, in business, at play, and at all times, whose word is to be relied on absolutely, who scorns whatever is mean. Such a man is like a great rock in a weary land, in whose shadow lesser, weaker men can gather and in his strength be made strong.

It appears that Pepys, the diarist, in order to atone for some juggling to avoid direct taxation, designed to charge himself with £1000, but, finding that no one else of his own station did so, he feared to appear singular, and abandoned his purpose. Stevenson's comment is, " One able merchant's countenance, and Pepys had dared to do an honest act ! Had he found one brave spirit properly recognised by society, he might have gone far as a disciple ! " Underneath the scorn, is there not a warning for us all ? We know not who may be watching us, in a dilemma betwixt the wrong they are ashamed of, and the right they lack the courage to do. If one upright character may turn the scale, what a potent thing the influence of even one may be ! It spreads, it perpetuates itself. Cheerfulness, faith, straightness—these are all contagious blessings.

" And they journeyed from Oboth, and pitched at Ije-Abarim, in the wilderness which is before Moab, toward the sun-rising."

(NUMBERS xxi. 11.)

XL

TOWARD THE SUNRISING

WHEN the writer of the Book of Numbers records that the Israelites " journeyed from Oboth and pitched at Ije-Abarim, in the wilderness which is before Moab, toward the sun-rising," all that he meant to convey, probably, was that the travellers held east. But his phrase means more than that, for it suggests to us a company of men making their way through a flat, uninspiring land, upheld by the hope of To-morrow Morning. The very words have poetry in them ! " Travelling in the wilderness, toward the sun-rising." That is THE way to travel, my brothers ! With the desert about us, as it is about us all, at times, yet with hopes fixed on what lies forward and beyond, and deliberately guiding our steps that way. That is true living ; that is the life of faith. I know not a more beautiful paraphrase of the Christian hope than this, " in the wilderness, but journeying toward the sun-rising."

This is the GLORIOUS way to travel. It is not

true to fact to say that " Life is a desert drear,"
though we sometimes sing words like these.
But neither is it true to say that Life is a picnic.
For the heart knoweth its own bitterness, and
each man has his burden to bear. Yet, whatever
the trouble be, the glorious way to take it, ay,
even with tears in one's eyes, is with one's face
toward the sunrising. Nothing can overcome
the man who persists in believing in To-morrow
Morning. The big, noble way to live, be the
darkness what it may, is to steer for the place
where the dawn ought to be. So it is that all
the heroes have won out in the end. They
followed their gleam doggedly, loyally, right
through the wilderness and on to the very
end.

To travel hopefully, making for the land we
cannot see, and the Love we have not scales
to measure, is to travel in the company of earth's
noblest pilgrims. Best of all, it is to travel in
the company of Jesus Himself ; for the glory
of His life, above its seeming failure, was its faith
and hope. As one who catches sight of some
far beacon marking the way home, He set His
face steadfastly to go to Jerusalem and " for the
joy that was set before Him endured the
Cross."

This is the HELPFUL way to travel. What a

great deal of good it does one to happen upon a cheery soul on life's highway of a morning! There are men whose greeting is a benediction; they radiate hopefulness and the promise of better things to come, as the sun scatters light and heat.

Stevenson has said that the man who looks at the silver lining in his cloud is a public benefactor, and that is true. For faith, remember, is infectious. You can catch it from some one else. The big, hearty soul, whose hope is in God, steadfast and immovable, draws weaker men toward the sunrising too.

Along this line also, Jesus brings new life to men. When we see that in a life as truly human as our own, there shone such faith in the Father's Love, such an assurance that beyond the darkness, past the Cross and death, there lay hope and light and victory, our hearts reach out to claim it as their faith. There are men whom that has drawn as nothing else could draw them, for whom even that alone marks Jesus as the Lord and Leader of their choice and sworn fealty. And, like R. W. Gilder's Galilean, they declare:—

> "If Jesus Christ is a man,—
>   And only a man,—I say
> That of all mankind I cleave to Him,
>   And to Him will I cleave alway.

"If Jesus Christ is a God,—
   And the only God,—I swear
I will follow Him through heaven and hell,
   The earth, the sea, and the air."

This is a STRENUOUS way to travel. I do not read that these Israelites longed for the sun-rising or gazed toward it, but that they journeyed in that direction. People who are not naturally hopeful sometimes find fault with the optimists, and say, It's easy for them to be hopeful. That is a mistake. There are times when it is not easy for anybody to be hopeful. But the Optimist is the man who holds for the sunrising, even when it is not easy.

It's not enough to sit still and admire the promise of the Dawn, as travellers in the East watch the mirage shimmering in the heat. The thing to do is to bend our lives that way, to work towards our faith, to live in the direction of the sunrising. And sometimes that is far from easy.

Even when the hope is dim and the vision blurred, however, we can still remain loyal to the old direction; and that is often the best way to get the old hope back again. It was a true and shrewd remark that Lady Blanche Balfour once made to a friend who confessed that, because of his doubts, he had given up the practice of prayer—" That is a mistake," said Lady Balfour; keep the frame and the picture will grow into it again!" Keep the frame. Point for the things you WISH to be true. Act as you would if you were sure of them. Even when you question whether the sun for you will ever rise again, lay your last course bravely for the dawn. " Then said Evangelist, pointing with his hand over a very wide field, Do you see yonder wicket gate ? The man said, No. Then said the other, Do you see yonder shining light ? He said, I think I do. Then said Evangelist, Keep that light in your eye, *and go up directly thereto*, so shalt thou see the gate."

This way of travelling has its REWARD. It has its reward here, for, as Evangelist told his pilgrim, the light grows clearer as one travels towards it. But it has its final reward also. As those who hunger and thirst after righteousness shall be filled, so they who travel toward the sunrising shall come to the full light at last. That is the sure word of the Evangel. There is no good thing a man desires, no blessing of God he covets, no high pure hope he follows though it be afar off, but he shall yet find, and enjoy, and come to, " some day, if not yet ; somewhere, if not here." With all your heart and with all your strength believe in God's sunrise, and, day by day, persuade your feet in that way, and you will arrive at last. For God's day is not like ours, morning and then night—It's " the evening and the morning" that make His Day, first the darkness, and then the dawn, first the Night and then the Day-break, when the shadows flee away

" And there were in the same country shepherds abiding in the field, keeping watch over their flock by night."

(LUKE ii. 8.)

" Now when Jesus was born in Bethlehem . . . there came wise men from the east to Jerusalem."

(MATTHEW ii. 1.)

XLI

THE SHEPHERDS, THE CHILD, AND THE WISE MEN

A MESSAGE FOR CHRISTMAS DAY

THE spell of Christmas has fallen again upon our busy world. All the year round, little as it thinks of it, that world pays its homage to the fact of Christ and His lowly cradle at Bethlehem; for there is not a newspaper or a cheque or a letter that does not carry a date upon it, and thereby bears its witness to Christ. The civilised world reckons its time from that first Christmas Day. Not only our friendships and our reading but even our commerce bears that hidden Name upon its records.

But who when he writes " 19— " ever thinks what these figures mean? To-day, however, it is different. The hum of industry has died down, the office and the shop are closed, there is a truce even in political affairs, and our world stands still for a little. In the busy year this is the hour of the Angels. In the tender mood that claims us to-day when we are touched by old memories, and the gladness of home, and the simple delights of the children, the angels and shepherds and the Christ-Child of the beautiful Old Story somehow do not seem so very far away. It were well for us surely to linger here in thought for a little while this morning.

It is strange, when one thinks of it, that the angel choir should have chosen some shepherds for their audience. One might have expected that the Good News of a Saviour's birth would be proclaimed first to the Church, that the foreshadowings of the Evangel would be revealed to some select company of holy men who waited for the coming of the Messiah. Instead of that, the message came to ordinary men at their daily calling, to representatives of the world's workers, to shepherds watching their flocks by night. Let that remind us again—what Christendom has again and again forgotten—that Christ refuses to be bound by any limits of class, or by any institution, no matter how useful. This is the Advent of a Universal Deliverer, a Saviour of men.

If there is any danger of us coming to think

that the Church has a monopoly of Christ, so that to be outside of it for whatever reason is to be far off from Him and beyond His reach, let us correct that tendency and learn a truer wisdom. God's Christmas Gift was to the world, to men and women, not merely to the devout and expectant, but to its humble, toiling millions. The Gospel was preached, by angels, first to the common people.

And not only so, but it was preached to men at their work. We are all very apt to regard the day's work and religion as things apart. Yet here at the very beginning, the message of the Evangel enters the sphere of daily duty and claims its hearing there, fit symbol of the fact that it comes to redeem the world's work and turn its toil to worship. And it is doing so, slowly, " not with observation." There is many a man to-day who offers God not only his spiritual homage, but also the tribute of his week's clean duty, whatever it may be, and believes that God accepts both. There is many a man at his desk or in the workshop who dares, since Christ has come, to count himself a co-worker with God. That man is justified. Duty and worship for the disciple are not things apart. It was to men at their work that our Religion's first word was spoken.

The world's Art has ever since loved to picture what it was the Shepherds saw when they came to the Stable of the Inn — in a rude stall, with beasts of the field lying around, a Jewish woman with a gentle face and wistful eyes that shone with a pure light like a star's. It was a woman and a little Child. Chiefly, it was a little Child.

This is something new in history. Not till this night had a child counted for much in the world's esteem. Men and women, their doings and their darings, their sacrifices and their sins —of these there are records plentiful enough, but of the child scarcely a single word. Before Christ came, it has been said, there were no children, and in its essential meaning the saying is true. But the wonder of that first Christmas has changed that. That God should stoop to men and come among them " as a little child " is the supreme glory of Childhood, a glory that is great enough to hallow all our children and sanctify our homes. Since Jesus lived, men and women have learned, what no one saw before, that there is nothing on earth that is more truly of Heaven than a little child. And this was the beginning of it all, for the prophecy of olden time had been fulfilled at last and a Child had become a Leader.

And so, fathers and mothers, it is right and proper that at this season especially you should bend down among the children and enter into their simple joys. Their transparent mysteries, the anticipated delights of awakening that rob the very darkness of its rest, their pleasure in giving and receiving, and all the revels of the season— let no detail be omitted, nor a drop of their happiness spilled out. Heed not the grumbler who complains of the confusion or the cost. For Christmas belongs to the children as it belongs to no one else. It is the birthday of the whole tribe, the anniversary of their coming to their kingdom. It is our opportunity too, who have been beholden to that leading many times for lessons in trust and self-forgetfulness, to pay back something of our debt.

> "O Thou, who wast a Child, and clung
>   Unto the Dream that never dies,
> Keep us, for all our blindness, young,
>   And make us, like Thy children, wise."

After the Shepherds came the Wise Men. Science followed in the steps of natural piety and worshipped at the same shrine. But how different were the paths by which they came! The shepherds saw no Star, though it had flamed above their heads the whole night through. Never an echo of angel voices reached the " starled wizards " from the East. But God was guiding both. That is the point, God was guiding

both. His City has gates on its east side as well
as on the west.

When one man tries to describe his most sacred
memories to another, shows him the place where
he had his vision of God, lets him see the book or
poem that has been as His living Word to him,
how often is that other surprised that any man
should see God in such a spot, or hear His Voice
in so ordinary a page of print ! At the very
place where our friend has beheld the glory of
the Lord, how often have we, like the knights in
Arthur's battle, " looking upwards, only seen the
mist " ?

Is not the lesson, then, for us all this blessed
season, Charity and again Charity ? Belittle no
man's star. Suspect not your brother's angel,
though the skies be silent for you. Let us keep
our Christmas in spirit by putting away from us
all uncharitableness. Some of us cannot hear
your angels, my brother—it may be because
our ears are dull. But God speed you on your
pilgrimage ! For us, we thank God, there is at
least His Star. But star-led or angel-led, let us
remember to-day at least, though we forget it
again too soon, that we are brethren in this
quest. For angel and star alike are the finger-
posts of God, and the paths meet at last at the
feet of Christ.

XLII

FORWARD !

A MESSAGE FOR THE NEW YEAR

WHEN the children of Israel were caught in a corner, with the Red Sea in front of them, and Egypt's chariots behind, it is not surprising that they should have acted like frightened sheep, utterly abandoned to terror. But when a sudden voice rang like a trumpet through their trembling ranks, bidding them go forward, the soul of the people awoke to life. They found that they had the courage to go forward. And when they did, they found that wonderful things happened. That call made them men, God's men. They learned, for the whole world, that to go bravely forward trusting in God is to give Him His chance.

There is a time to stand still, doubtless ; and there certainly is a time to wait in prayer upon God for His help and guidance. But these stages only bear their fruit when we pluck up courage and go forward. Nothing can happen till then. God has no chance to answer our prayers till then. From that far day in the annals of Israel, to this, that splendid rallying cry has been the very Word of God to His people whenever they fall despondent and fear what is to come—" Speak unto the children of Israel that they go forward." It is His Word to us to-day, as He opens before us the gate of another year.

Those who are facing difficult tasks, duties that frighten or responsibilities that weigh heavy, need to have their blood stirred and their courage stiffened by being told in God's name to go straight up to the thing, whatever it be, and do it ! It may be a difficult interview, or some apology to be made, something in business to-morrow, or merely some halting and long-delayed purpose after what is really good. You know best what your particular Red Sea is. You have stood still and looked at it. Perhaps you have prayed about it, but it is still there, God's ordained obstacle in your way. Well, His Word to you to-day, my brother, is Forward March ! The time for prayer is past. Give God a chance to answer it, now. And let me tell you, that, as sure as He is in His Heaven, if He has planted this thing in your way, if you come to it by the call of Duty, if He has led you to this Red Sea of yours, He'll bring you through it somehow, if only you go forward. Things happen, wonders happen—aye, miracles happen, when we go forward, trusting in God. Gates open, apparently of their own accord. Mountains of difficulty dwindle into climbable slopes. The very sea has a path through it, after all. Forward, then, with your trust in God, no matter what is to come. It is a brave man's favourite direction even with danger in front. It is the Christian's only direction, when God and Duty have pointed out the way.

> " Behind him lay the grey Azores,
>   Behind, the gates of Hercules ;
> Before him not the ghost of shores,
>   Before him only shoreless seas.
>
> The good mate said, ' Now must we pray,
>   For lo ! the very stars are gone !
> Brave Admiral, speak, what shall I say ? '
>   ' Why say, " Sail on ! Sail on ! and on ! " ' '

Further, there is a message here for all perplexed and doubting souls. Even for them there is a way out. And the way is just right forward ! What happens, for example, as a general rule to the man who has lost his faith in prayer ? He stops praying. Is it not so ? He gives the habit up. Whereas his way of deliverance is to go on. Even though I am in doubt, he asks, as to whether God hears me ? Yes, even then. You will never learn the truth about prayer if

Q

you give up the practice, no matter what your doubts or your darkness be. And more—you will come to have no desire to learn. But pray on, and the faith and the justification will surely come again.

To the man or woman for whom the faith of God's fatherhood has become eclipsed, the way out also is right forward, living, helping, healing, loving, as a son would wish to do, if Fatherhood were a fact. If the Christ-light by which you chose your direction in days gone by has become troubled, keep on that very road still. Eclipses do not last for ever. Forward is the direction for the doubter, even though meantime it be forward in the dark.

Again, this is a message for every soldier in the Army of Christ. Moods come to the most strenuous when they sit down and try to reckon up the prospects of success. Despondency is apt to find them then too easy a prey. There are always the croakers, too, who say that Christ's day is past and His Church is being left behind. And, though Time has refuted these prophecies again and again, one is apt to give them a ready ear when one is weary. Some months since, the *Times* re-printed, from its issue of 100 years ago, an advertisement of a book " On the Impending Ruin of the British Empire," by Hector

Campbell. Whereupon it was cheerfully pointed out by somebody that the writer and the printer are both dead, the very street where it had been published has disappeared, and the British Empire remains, growing yet ! That's the way to talk ! And specially and safely is it the way to talk about God's Kingdom.

Short pessimism, as somebody has called it, may be pardoned occasionally to a Christian man, that is, he may question whether some particular fragment of Christian activity is likely to be successful in a short space of time. For we are like weavers, working with only the underside of the web visible, and

> " We may not see how the right side looks,
> We can only weave and wait."

But long pessimism—hopelessness regarding the final issues—is not permissible. One cannot be a Christian and admit that some day the spirit of this world will conquer the spirit of Christ. This wave or that one, as you watch them on the shore, may disappoint you. But the tide comes in at last for all that. " All my days," said Macaulay, the historian, " I have seen nothing but progress, and heard of nothing but decay." God is as willing as ever to deliver those who put their trust in Him. The Name of Christ still casts out devils from men's lives.

It only seems that the glory has departed because we stand shivering on the brink of the great new tasks to which God is calling us to-day. Let us go bravely forward, and the sea will be divided for us again. All God asks is that we give Him a chance; and He does not get that till we rise up and catch hold.

Yet harder, sometimes, than attempting new tasks is to continue loyally at the old ones. At whiles our hands fall slack, and we ask, maybe, what we should do. So did one of those brave fellows with Captain Scott's Antarctic party ask, when his feet were so badly frostbitten that walking was an agony, and yet to halt was certain death. And the answer that he got sends a thrill through every too-easily-discouraged soldier among us, "Slog on! Just slog on!" It is THE answer, THE watchword for every one of us in any campaign of our Master's. It is a moral certainly that nothing will happen so long as we are halting. But to go bravely forward, relying on God, is to invite the miracle. To slog on, in God's expeditions at least, is to win out right in the end.

> "They sailed. They sailed. Then spoke the mate,
>   ' This mad sea shows his teeth to-night,
> He curls his lip, he lies in wait
>   With lifted teeth as if to bite.

" ' Brave Admiral, say but one good word,
What shall we do when Hope is gone ?
The words leaped as a leaping sword,
' Sail on ! Sail on ! Sail on, and on ! ' "

So our Admiral calls to every one of us voyaging on His business. And HE will surely see to it that we get to port.